"Your Perception IS Your Reality"
The Truth about Hypnosis

By Michael C. White, C.Ht.

To April

Love Mike

First Edition
Copyright© 2010 by Michael C. White

All rights reserved. No part of this book
may be reproduced in any form, electronic or
mechanical, including photocopy, recording, or
any information storage or retrieval system,
without permission in writing from the author.

iii

DEDICATION

I dedicate this book to my wife Nicole and my sons Anthony and Charlie for their patience with my obsessive pursuit of my passion for knowledge.

And to my brother Chris, whose shared insanity helps to keep me sane.

Acknowledgment

A special thanks to the members of the Katy Hypnosis Group in Katy and Houston Texas, for their participation in the development of the materials for this book and for their support of the growth and development of hypnosis in general. And a very special thanks to my fellow hypnotists and colleagues, Steve Solek, Kaushik Nag, Shawn Erwin, Julius Williams, and Stage Hypnotist, Mentalist and Magician Extraordinaire Robert Berry.

And an extra very special thank you to J Walker for his superb editing skills. You sir are greatly appreciated.

Contents

Introduction

First of all, I would like to thank you for purchasing this book. Your curiosity about hypnosis and your desire to gather more information proves that there is continued growth in the field of hypnosis and hypnotherapy.

I composed this book with the intention of helping to guide the average individual, with a general curiosity about hypnosis, through the process of becoming educated in the hypnotic process; and then further into how to hypnotize others as well as how to use hypnosis to help others improve their lives.

There has been a lot of new discovery in the field of hypnosis, and there is still so much more to learn and discover. I have worked very hard to ensure that the information provided in this text is as thorough and complete as possible. While we'll go fairly broadly into the field of hypnosis, there are some areas where we will also travel fairly deeply and get into the specific nuts and bolts of technique and practice. Consider this a primer for your continued study of hypnosis and hypnotherapy.

It's impossible to fit all there is to learn about hypnosis into a single text, and I encourage you to seek out and discover as many other resources as possible to deepen your understanding and overall knowledge about the phenomenon of hypnosis, and the field of hypnosis and hypnotherapy for the betterment of yourself and of all mankind.

The internet is an extremely rich resource for learning hypnosis. There are endless sources of information, in text and video format, to learn new techniques as well as to gain deeper understanding of the application of hypnosis for vocational and avocational self-improvement, as well as clinical applications of hypnotherapy.

I have endeavored to write this book in a tone that is easy to read and comprehend, abandoning the temptation to get very technical and clinical on the subject in exchange for an approach whose purpose is to increase understanding and therefore, broader acceptance of hypnosis as a valid and effective means of self-improvement.

My hope is that, by the time you finish reading this book, you will realize that hypnosis is an integral part of our day-to-day lives. We can't escape it because it is part of us, and it is intermingled in all learning and communication.

Hypnosis is not "mysticism", or "the occult", or anything to fear: it's a natural ability that we all have, and a process that we tap into for many different scenarios. By understanding this natural process for communicating with our own subconscious, we can realize that we have more control over our lives and our futures than we may have previously thought. Our perception IS our reality and we can change our perception of the world by changing our beliefs, eliminating our fears and negative self-talk, and striving to make continuous positive improvements in our lives.

Disclaimer

All of the information provided in this book is intended for general education about hypnosis. Be sure to check the legislation in your area, pertaining to the use of hypnosis, before attempting to practice these techniques with others.

Although, as of the writing of this book, there is no licensing body for hypnotists overall, there are several areas that restrict the use of hypnosis, as a therapeutic tool, by anyone other than a licensed medical professional, whether that be a doctor of medicine, or a psychologist. So again, verify with your local, state and federal legislation as to any guidelines or restrictions around the use of hypnosis with individuals, or in public displays.

With that being said, your decision to use the techniques and processes described in this book are your individual choice and the author and publisher of this book take no responsibility for the effectiveness or outcome of the use of the materials provided within.

The author encourages anyone interested in using hypnosis for vocational, avocational or therapeutic use to ensure that they have adequate training and practical application practice before using hypnosis in a professional capacity.

First, a little background

I don't want to bore you with a long dissertation about the history of hypnosis and its key players; there are plenty of resources on the internet to gain a thorough and complete history of hypnosis, and its main characters. My intention here is just to give a summary of the history of Hypnosis, simply to provide a foundation for discussion of hypnosis in general.

Hypnosis is not a new development; it has been part of humanity since very early development of the species. In pre-historic times, when a person was threatened, he had two choices: he could stand and fight, or he could run away. As societies developed, and humanity started living in larger villages, towns and communities, it became less and less acceptable to fight or run away, so we had to develop new ways of engaging in "fight or flight". The human psyche developed the hypnotic state as a mechanism to allow us to escape "inwardly" to deal with situations of high anxiety. More about this later.

Ancient History

If you study history very closely, you will find many examples of hypnosis being demonstrated. From the Ancient Egyptians and Greeks, who had "sleep" temples, to various forms of ancient (and modern) religions and cults who used (and in some cases still do) what we now know to be hypnotic techniques, to communicate their teachings, and sometimes influence and persuade their followers.

Story Telling

One of the earliest examples of hypnosis is story telling. As a means of group communication, stories were used to communicate information to the masses. Members of the community would gather to hear tales of hunting grounds, areas or situations of peril, legends, etc. Before written history, stories were the only way that knowledge was passed down from generation to generation. Often times, these stories were not only told, but also illustrated through song, dance, ritual, paintings etc., allowing the audience to experience the stories more richly, by engaging more of their senses. As you will learn, these are all ways of bypassing the critical factor and engaging the subconscious, thereby creating a hypnotic state for deeper absorption of the information being presented.

You might be saying "Come on, now. How can telling a story be hypnosis?" Well, that's a very good question. Have you ever read a story or article and experienced an emotional response? Become sad or happy, or laughed at something funny you read? Where did these emotions come from? This is just ink on paper: cryptic symbols that we have come to associate to words, and words that describe situations and scenarios. How can they have an "emotional" effect on us?

Emotions are a subconscious action. When we read, the words and writings themselves have no inherent meaning, other than what we give them. We have created "associations" to words that we have learned to "identify" and now we can read or hear those words and create images in our minds. The associations to these "symbols on paper" bring up related memories or imagined images, and those images or memories elicit emotional responses.

This ability to change "emotional states" is a mild hypnotic process. We can experience it while reading, listening to the radio, watching TV or movies. Whenever we experience an emotional response in conjunction with an experience, we create new neuropathways which allow us to recall that experience more easily. You'll learn how this very powerful and influential technique is used in everything from religion to advertising and marketing.

Religion

All religions (and especially cults) utilize hypnotic techniques as a means of indoctrinating their followers and re-enforcing their teachings in order to maintain and grow their congregations. Now, I realize that this is a very controversial subject, and it's not my intention to persuade or dissuade anyone concerning their spirituality or beliefs. I understand the need for religious faith for many people and I respect each person's right to believe (or not believe) in whatever they want. My intent here is to simply point out the use of hypnotic techniques in religion as a highly effective means of distributing teachings.

If you break down the techniques used, you can begin to understand their power to influence. The use of large temples and churches ornately decorated with figures of deities, saints and gods, and saturated with symbolism. Large vaulted ceilings and vast expanses of space, designed to make visitors feel small and insignificant. Authority figures dressed in special uniforms, delivering the teachings from a raised location, usually in front of a large symbol of their faith (this positioning of the religious leader, in front of the symbol, while teaching the "word", is designed to create an association between the deliverer of the message and the "originator" of the message).

Even the sermons themselves are delivered in a fashion that is designed to fractionate the subconscious (more on fractionation later) in order to induce deeper states for stronger and more deeply ingrained learning, and to alter or mold the "core beliefs" of the followers. We'll discuss the power of "core beliefs" later on.

Many of the same speech delivery techniques utilized by religious leaders are also incorporated by motivational speakers and political speakers, because of their effectiveness in bypassing the critical factor to penetrate deep into the listener's subconscious for deeper learning, understanding and retention. And of course, the multi-billion dollar marketing and advertising industry is saturated with hypnotic language and technique, all designed to persuade us into buying whatever product or service is being presented.

Hypnotic phenomenon can account for many "miraculous" events, such as healing springs, statues and sites, and the "laying on of hands" by individuals with high religious status. Even in modern times, the Placebo effect encountered in many clinical trials can be attributed to the power of the subconscious mind.

Recent History

In more recent history, we see the formalization of hypnosis begin to develop. In the mid 1700's, Franz Anton Mesmer, a Viennese physician, achieved many spectacular "healings" through what he perceived to be an invisible "magnetic fluid", but was later determined to be the power of hypnosis and the subconscious mind. The term "Mesmerism" and the concept of "Animal Magnetism" are tied to the work developed by Dr. Mesmer. A commission, ordered by Louis XVI, of which one of the members was none other than Benjamin Franklin, later determined that there was no invisible magnetic field at work and that the people were being cured by no more than their own minds.

In 1841, the term "Hypnosis" was coined by a Manchester surgeon, Dr. James Braid, who described the hypnotic subjects as seeming to be asleep (*hypnosis* derives from a Greek word meaning "sleep"). He later tried to change the name to "Monoideism", once he realized that the subjects weren't actually asleep, but in fact were in a deep state of

6

relaxed, hyper suggestibility, but the new term didn't catch on, so we still refer to it as "Hypnosis" to this very day.

Hypnosis was used throughout the psychological profession for much of the 1800s, until Dr. Sigmund Freud abandoned it in favor of psychoanalytic techniques. This delivered a devastating blow to the use of hypnosis, and the practice of hypnosis may well have drifted off into obscurity, if it had not been for the use of hypnosis by stage performers, to amaze and entertain their audiences.

Modern Hypnosis

The use of hypnosis by the psychological community in the early part of the twentieth century was limited to inducing relaxation in behavioral therapies, for anxiety, and to induce behavioral change. Milton Hyland Erickson, known as the father of modern hypnotherapy, is probably one of the most prominent pioneers in hypnosis as a therapeutic tool and is chiefly responsible for the resurgence of hypnosis as a means of effecting real, permanent change in people's lives.

In the 1950's, Milton H. Erickson was key in getting the acceptance of Hypnosis by the American Medical Association. Since then, there have been many pioneers in the field of Hypnosis and Hypnotherapy, and Neural-Linguistic Programming (NLP is a modeling technique, but can also be used as a form of waking or conversational hypnosis, although some will argue that it's not hypnosis at all), and I'll be sharing some of these breakthroughs and innovations with you in this book.

What Is Hypnosis?

The United States Government defines hypnosis as follows:

"Hypnosis is the bypass of the critical factor of the mind and the acceptance of acceptable selective thinking."

So what does this mean exactly? Let's break it down:
"the bypass of the critical factor". What is the "critical factor", and why do we need to bypass it? We'll break this down in more detail when we get into the "Model of the Mind", but for now you can think of the "critical factor" as a filter or "middle man" of sorts, that controls what information gets into your subconscious. With hypnosis, you can bypass the "critical factor" and talk directly to the subconscious, thereby cutting out the "middle man", so to speak.

The *"acceptance of acceptable selective thinking"* refers to the suggestions that are given to the subconscious by a hypnotist, or by oneself in the case of self-hypnosis (we'll discuss the difference in a minute). What makes a suggestion "acceptable" is based on a person's "core beliefs" and whether or not the suggestion poses some sort of threat to the subject.

How Hypnosis Developed

No one really knows for certain how the hypnotic state developed in humans, but the generally accepted theory is that it developed out of necessity, in parallel with the development of structured society, as a means of "fight or flight" for protection of the human psyche. Just as some animals can fake death to avoid predators, early man may have developed similar skills to escape danger, or control pain from injury, or to achieve altered states of consciousness in order to communicate more effectively with their world and their environment. Many of these "special" skills have been lost to modern man, but the hypnotic state and our ability to move in and out of it remains intact.

As humans developed, they learned to increase their tolerance levels and control the instinct to slip into primitive fight/flight responses. The "fight" response was controlled by developing the "Reaction" vs. "Action" syndrome, so that when threatened we began developing nervous anxiety and tension, then "Reaction" would take place and we would seek out physical ways of dealing with the stress, like exercise.

At other times, when threatened and we felt the urge to flee, the "flight" response was controlled by developing the "Repression" vs. "Depression" syndrome. Choosing to withdraw, taking everything inside (Repression), or escaping into fantasy or sleep (Depression).

When we become too overwhelmed by something, the environment, work, information, or physical threat, we may still revert back to primitive fight/flight responses. The subconscious takes over; our heart beats faster; blood pressure rises; blood is forced from our organs into our muscles; the pupils dilate, etc.; this is the sympathetic nervous system at work. Once the threat has passed, the parasympathetic nervous system kicks in, bringing everything back to normal (Homeostasis).

When we realize that we can't handle the overload we slip into a depressed, apathetic state of hyper suggestibility. Hypnosis is created by similar overloading processes, but in a positive, controlled situation.

The hypnotic state is a natural state that the mind goes into automatically. In fact, we go in and out of hypnosis multiple times in a day. Two times are for certain, that period just before we wake up in the morning, and just as we are falling asleep at night, however, because we can't tell when we are moving from a normal conscious state into hypnosis, we are generally unaware of it. With that said, let's discuss some myths and misconceptions about hypnosis.

Myths and Misconceptions about Hypnosis

Hollywood movies and television have done a horrible job of portraying hypnosis realistically. In fact, most of what you see on TV and in film, pertaining to hypnosis, is all wrong. Here are some commonly held beliefs about hypnosis, followed by the truth:

"Only stupid or weak minded individuals can be hypnotized."

In actuality, the more intelligent you are and the stronger your will is, the easier it is for you to enter the hypnotic state.

"Only a select portion of the population can be hypnotized."

The truth is, anyone of normal intelligence and brain function can be hypnotized, and as stated earlier, has been in hypnosis many, many times during their lives. The exceptions are people with deep-seeded psychosis; people with certain brain injuries or defects; and very young, infant children, and the only reason these children can't be hypnotized, is because they are already in a state of hyper suggestibility, so you can't hypnotize them, because they are already there.

"You're unconscious or asleep when you are hypnotized."

The reality is you are completely awake and fully aware of what's going on while in hypnosis. In fact, many of your senses are heightened while in the hypnotic state. You hear more clearly, you can see better, you feel everything; you're just in a very relaxed state of hyper suggestibility.

Most people that are guided into hypnosis are done so with their eyes closed, so it looks like they're asleep, but in fact, they are not. If they were asleep, they wouldn't be able to hear anything; therefore they wouldn't be able to follow the hypnotist's suggestions.

In fact, eye closure isn't even necessary to generate the hypnotic state. Conversational hypnosis works on this principle, so do marketing and advertising. You're not asleep when engaged in a movie, book or TV show (unless it has a really boring plot). Hypnotists generally use eye closure for two reasons: to help relax the subject, and to add additional overload by taking away one of the subjects senses.

"The hypnotist can make you do whatever they want you to do."

This is the biggest misconception of them all. A hypnotist can't hypnotize you against your will, and they can't make you do anything in hypnosis that you wouldn't normally do, given the right circumstances, or which violates your "core beliefs". Unlike events portrayed in popular films and TV shows, a hypnotist can't hypnotize you and make you rob a bank or kill someone, unless your belief is that these things are ok to do, and it's something you would normally do, but this isn't an issue for the vast majority of the population, since most people believe (even if only at the subconscious level) these activities to be wrong and therefore would reject such suggestions and come out of hypnosis.

"You might get stuck in hypnosis."

This is physically impossible. Sometimes, when people are deeply hypnotized, they reach a state of such deep, blissful relaxation, that they don't want to emerge from it, but even if that were to happen, without the hypnotist there talking to you, you would eventually drift off into a normal sleep, and eventually wake up like you always do.

Hetero vs. Self-Hypnosis

When you're hypnotized by someone else, this is known as Hetero Hypnosis. It's typically accomplished by disorganizing the inhibitory processes and overloading the conscious mind with message units, creating a controlled state of anxiety and triggering the "escape" into the hypnotic state.

Self-hypnosis, as you probably guessed, is when you put yourself into a state of hypnosis. This is usually accomplished by focusing the mind to achieve a state of enhanced focus and relaxation.

The popular "self-hypnosis" self-help recordings that many people buy are actually hetero hypnosis tapes, because even though the hypnotist is not present physically, it is still their words and voice that guide you into hypnosis.

Overt vs. Covert Hypnosis

Within Hetero Hypnosis, there are two approaches: "Overt" and "Covert". Overt hypnosis is when the person being hypnotized knows you are hypnotizing them. For example, when a person volunteers to participate in a stage hypnosis show, they know that the hypnotist is going to hypnotize them. The same is true for someone going to a hypnotherapist, it's understood that hypnosis is going to occur.

Covert hypnosis is when the person being hypnotized doesn't realize that hypnosis is being used. For example, in many advertising, commercials and sales pitches, hypnotic techniques are utilized for persuasion, but the recipient, the person being "sold" to, often times does not realize that they are being influenced by way of hypnotic techniques.

A Rose by Any Other Name

Hypnosis and the hypnotic state can be achieved in a variety of ways; the following are some of the more commonly experienced means.

Environmental Hypnosis

The hypnotic state can be triggered by your environment. The most commonly known is "Highway Hypnosis". Have you ever been driving somewhere and found yourself so deep in thought that you arrive at your destination with no recollection of the drive to get there? Or, perhaps you were driving down a familiar stretch of road, with the intention of going one place, only to miss your exit or take a different exit, because that's where you normally go? These are both examples of "highway hypnosis".

What happens? Where does your mind go? Who was driving? The truth is you were in an altered state of consciousness, deep in your own thoughts, so your subconscious just "took the driver's seat" for a while. Chances are you were driving very safely and very carefully while in that state. Had a real emergency come up, you would have snapped back into conscious awareness and dealt with the situation as needed.

Other examples of "environmental hypnosis" could be situations where people find themselves in a traumatic or highly stressful situation, unable to make reasonable decisions on their own, so they follow whomever seems to know what he is doing. This explains the "mob" mentality, during times of high emotional stress, where normal everyday people will find themselves looting, or following the instructions of someone they normally wouldn't, just because they themselves are overwhelmed by the situation and will follow the example or instructions of others, basically following the "path of least resistance" because they have lost sight of their own path.

Meditation

Meditation is a form of self-hypnosis, the practice of which allows an individual to achieve increasingly deeper and profound levels of introspection and focus. Meditation is practiced by many spiritual people as a way to try and achieve self-enlightenment. It is also practiced by many people as a way to deal with day-to-day stress, as well as to make

13

positive changes within themselves and to increase their own self-awareness.

The "Zone"

The "Zone" achieved by many high performance athletes, during practice or competition, is a form of self-hypnosis, where the athlete develops a sort of "tunnel vision" where the only thing in their conscious awareness is the task at hand. This state of mind is a very common practice in martial arts. It allows the martial artist to think through the seemingly impossible and accomplish astonishing feats, like breaking boards and bricks with their bare hands and feet. The same principle is at play during fire walks and other displays of "mind over matter" feats.

In the next chapter, we'll break down the logical model of the mind and explain the mechanics of the hypnotic process.

Model of the Mind

This section will get a little "fuzzy" because of some medical terms used to describe the brain anatomy in play with the various parts of the model being discussed, so I'll apologize in advance for that. However, I believe this to be necessary, so that we understand that there is real hard science at the very foundation of hypnosis. Too often, our profession gets relegated to the realm of the occult, mysticism, or new age theology, however, there is real science behind what we hypnotists do, and it is my goal here to bring that science to the forefront.

There are many different models of the mind out there. I happen to like the one developed by the Hypnosis Motivation Institute, founded by Dr. John Kappas, so I have adopted their model for our discussion.

Theory of the Mind

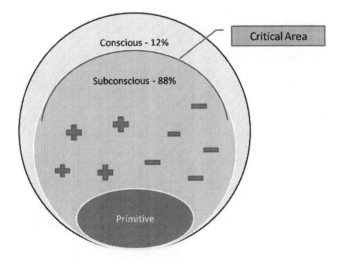

Figure 1: The Theory of Mind

The Primitive Mind

The primitive mind, also known as the reptilian brain, which is made up of the brain stem, medulla oblongata, Pons, and the limbic system, controls the autonomic functions (temperature, respiration, heart rate, etc.) along with the sympathetic and parasympathetic systems, which are the "fight/flight" systems of the brain and are controlled by the amygdala within the limbic system.

When we are threatened, the sympathetic system kicks in, releasing adrenalin into the blood stream and restricting blood flow to the extremities, preparing us for fight or flight. Once the threat has passed, the parasympathetic system reverses the process, allowing the body to achieve homeostasis, a balanced state.

You have probably felt the effects of the sympathetic system when someone cut you off on the freeway, or you were nearly in an accident. All of a sudden, your heart is racing, you're totally alert and reacting quickly to find the appropriate escape route, then, after the danger has passed, the parasympathetic system kicks in and your heart rate begins to slow, your breathing returns to normal and you calm down.

The amygdala is always on alert, looking out for danger, so that it can react quickly. You may be aware of the fact that when you accidentally place your hand down on a hot surface, you'll find that you jerk your hand back; just seconds before it registers to your conscious that you are being burned…that's the amygdala in action. The amygdala works with the parietal lobe (middle lobe), which controls motor perception and sensory perception. These two perception centers sit side by side, to ensure that there is no delay between what we sense and how we respond to it.

The Subconscious Mind

When we're born, the primitive mind is pretty much all we have. The rest of the mind is fairly blank (in a cognitive sense). All of the neurons are there; they just don't have any connections. For example, we don't know how to "see" when we're born. All of the information is coming in, but we have no basis of reference in order to process the visual stimulus and create identifiable images.

We learn through identification and association, and through repetition. Frequent exposure to the same information, over a period of time, begins to "etch" new neuropathways in our brain and once those pathways are formed, then the information becomes "known" to us. In figure 1, the pluses and minuses represent "knowns" to the subconscious mind. A known can be either a positive experience (plus sign) or negative experience (minus sign) depending on the experience we have and the emotional response connected to it.

For example, if a child is exposed to a kitten, and that kitten is playful and cuddly, then the child learns to "know" that kittens are good, and it's a positive experience. On the other hand, if another child is exposed to a kitten and, perhaps, that kitten doesn't want to be played with that day, so the kitten scratches the child, that child learns to "know" that kittens are bad, and it's a negative experience. Similar scenarios, but two very different experiences. This is how we learn and how we develop associations from our learning experiences, so that they can be identified later on.

How are neuropathways created?

Information enters the brain through our senses, which are controlled in the frontal lobe of the brain, where this sensory information is then processed by the cerebral cortex. The information enters the neurons from the synapse as a chemical signal, which is picked up by the dendrites of a neuron. These chemicals are converted into electrical signals within the nucleus of the neuron and then converted back into chemical signals and passed back into the synapse through the neuron's axons, where it is picked up by the dendrites of other neurons that are looking for the chemicals being released.

When this chemical link is established, the receiving neuron begins to move its dendrite closer to the transmitting neuron's axon. The more frequently the signal is transmitted and received, the faster the dendrite moves and the closer it gets, so that the chemical signal can be transmitted and picked up quicker. So the thing to understand here is that **"neurons that fire together, wire together"** and presto, we have a new neuropathway. Now, these neuropathways can be very complex, branching off into many sub-trees and branches, wiring together, experiences with memories, feelings, smells, sounds, sights, etc., each of which could have equally complex pathways to other experiences, and so on.

The Subconscious mind, which is basically everything outside of our conscious awareness, including the primitive mind, makes up approximately 88% of the total mind. Forgive me as I pass back and forth between the physical anatomy of the brain and the logical concept of the mind, hopefully you are seeing where these pieces fit together.

The subconscious mind is always active (even when we are sleeping) processing information, making new connections and associations, and influencing our conscious decisions.

The Critical Factor

Until about the age of 8 or 9, our minds are completely open, taking in all information without any criticism (this is why children are so gullible) because we are experiencing most of our world for the first time and therefore creating new associations and identifications.

Around the age of 8 or 9, we begin to develop the ability to critically analyze the information coming in and begin to compare it to information we already "know" to decide whether or not to accept the information or reject it outright.

So where is the "critical factor"? Here's what we believe: the brain is split into two halves, and in between these two halves is a mesh of nerve fibers called the corpus callosum, which is responsible for connecting the right and left brain. Riding along the top of the corpus callosum is the cingulated gyrus and, in the frontal lobe of the brain, the anterior cingulated gyrus is where scientists believe that information is filtered before being processed by the cerebral cortex. We believe that this is where the "critical factor" resides.

The "critical factor" resides halfway in the conscious mind and halfway in the subconscious mind and acts sort of like the bouncer at a club. When new information is presented to the mind, the critical factor asks "Do you have ID?", basically checking to see if the information has an existing associated identification. If not, then it doesn't let it in. If it does, then the velvet rope is lifted and all is cool.

Information from all of our senses bombards the conscious mind all day long. When message units enter the conscious mind, they move into the conscious part of the critical area, where they accumulate and sit, waiting to be processed. This is what causes "mental fatigue". We all have a threshold for the number of message units we can tolerate, but that threshold is different for everyone and can change over time. Overloading a person's threshold for message units is one of the processes used to induce hypnosis.

The Conscious Mind

The human mind receives about 400 Billion bits of information per second, but we are only consciously aware of about 2,000 bits at any given time. The conscious mind is the reasoning, analytical mind; it's the part of the mind that we associate our waking state to, and it makes up approximately 12% of the mind.

How do we know that the conscious mind is only 12% and that the subconscious mind makes up the other 88%? Well, if you think about all the things that we are experiencing at any given moment, only a small portion of that is in our conscious awareness. For example, only because I mention it now, you may find yourself aware of the chair you're sitting on, or your clothes touching your skin, or the hum of the lights, or other background noises around you. If we had to continuously be aware of and monitor all of these bits of information, and more, it would drive us mad, but the subconscious mind does it for us, with no complaints, allowing our conscious mind to attend to those things that are eminently important to us at the current moment.

The Reticular Activating System

A part of the limbic system that helps us to prioritize what we focus on is the Reticular Activating System. It can be activated in a couple of ways, and can bring things into our awareness that we normally wouldn't notice, like when we buy a new car, that we swear we have never seen before, and then drive off the lot, only to realize that it seems like everyone is driving that car. Now that the new car is part of our "known" associated identification, the reticular activating system allows it into our awareness.

This system can also obscure things from our awareness as well. If we expect something to be in one place, and it's actually somewhere else, we may not even detect its presence until it's brought to our attention. For example, have you ever been asked by your mother or spouse to get something from the pantry or refrigerator, and when you go to look for it, you can't find it, so you exclaim "we're out", only to have your mother or spouse come in, and with the pointing of their "magic" finger, show you the item that has been in front of you the entire time?

What happened? Did they actually make the item materialize from thin air? Perhaps, but the more likely scenario is that you expected it to be in the first place you looked, and then when it wasn't, you said to yourself "we don't have any". Then you looked in the second place and again, you said to yourself "we don't have any". This may occur several times, repeating each time that "we don't have any" to the point that you convince your subconscious that it is not there and you develop a "scotoma" or mental "blind spot" where the item is no longer "visible" to you because you are blocking the visual signals to your brain.

We do this to ourselves all the time, and not only with the salt and pepper shaker; we do this with opportunities, relationships, ideas, experiences, etc. We develop "blind spots" in our lives and experiences, which keep us from the things we really want, because we spend too much time focusing on the things we don't want.

Hypnosis can help us to "raise the veil" off of these mental blind spots, allowing us access to resources which, although they have been available to us all along, have been hidden from us, because of these mental blind spots.

Why "will power" often fails

"Will Power" is a process of the conscious mind. Have you ever noticed that some things you can give up without any trouble, but other things (things you really enjoy but you "know" are not good for you) like chocolate, or caffeine, you try to give up, only to find that, within a short period of time, you're back to consuming it again? Why is that? Why can't we just make up our minds to "quit" something and just do it? Why are some things so difficult to give up, while others take no effort at all?

Paul Scheele uses a great analogy to explain why "will power" often fails: If your conscious mind is 15 inches, then your subconscious mind is 15 miles. So when you try to use "will power" to quit a habit, you have the 15 miles (the 88% which is the subconscious mind) working against the 15 inches (the 12% conscious mind).

The things you can quit without effort have very little emotion attached to them and therefore little or no benefit. However, those things that give you pleasure, or that "seem" to give you resources to overcome issues, like stress, depression, sadness, etc., those habits have strong emotional attachments and therefore are controlled by the subconscious mind, which is stronger than the conscious mind.

Consider this scenario: You make a "conscious" decision to quit eating cake, relying on your "will power" to enforce your decision. So, with your "will power" fully engaged, you go to a friend's birthday party. Everything is going great, then, here comes the cake. You hear everyone around you praising the cake, commenting on how good it looks and how they can't wait to bite into it, but you have "resolved" not to eat, so you resist...for a while. Then something happens. You start to rationalize "It's a special occasion" or "It's my friend's birthday, one little piece won't kill me." Then you justify it with "I'll start my new diet tomorrow. And now, you're eating cake.

What happened? Why did you break your vow of "cake" abstinence? Well, this is what's going on inside of your mind. The "conscious" mind says "I'm not going to eat cake." This message is passed on to the critical factor, which in turn tells the "subconscious" mind "he says he's not going to eat cake, do we want to accept this suggestion?" Then the "subconscious" mind looks through all of your past behavior and says "Let me see, our records show that he loves cake. He had cake last year, he had cake last month, and as a matter of fact, he had cake yesterday. I think he wants to eat this cake...suggestion rejected."

The 12% conscious mind, is trying to override the 88% subconscious mind, but is simply overpowered, especially in situations where there are positive emotions or secondary gain benefits associated with the activity or behavior that you are trying to resist.

There is also an embedded suggestion in the phrase "I don't want to eat cake." Two things are going on here. First, the mind has to see you eating cake, before it can see you "not" eating cake. The second thing is a process whereby the mind has a tendency to drop the negative out of a sentence and only accept the positive, so "I don't want to eat cake" becomes "I want to eat cake." So, the lesson here is **"what you resist about you persists about you."** So, when trying to change behavior or habit, focus on the behavior or outcome that you "want" versus what you "don't want" and the self-suggestions will work more in your favor.

Suggestibility

Suggestibility can be described as how the mind learns and communicates information.

Direct vs. Indirect Suggestibility

It's generally agreed, in the hypnosis field, that there are two types of suggestibility: direct and indirect. Direct suggestible people receive information very directly, by that I mean they take information at face value. For example, if you were to say to a direct suggestible individual "You look great today!", they would feel good about your comment and take it to mean just what it states "I look great today."

Indirect suggestible people receive information through inferred meaning. For example, if you were to say to an indirect suggestible individual "You look great today!", they would immediately look for some underlying meaning. They may even respond with the question "What's so special about today? Are you saying I didn't look great yesterday?"

Now these are examples of extremes. In reality, we are a combination of both: we are able to take information in directly and indirectly. However, one suggestibility type is typically more dominant than the other, for about 70% of the population. There is, however, a small percentage of the population who are equally direct and indirect in their suggestibility. These individuals are known as somnambulists and can achieve great success, or succumb to great failure, depending on their environment and the influence it has on them. If they learn early on that they have this ability to pull information in from so many different forms, then they can learn to control the flow of information to their ultimate benefit.

Dr. John G. Kappas, founder of the Hypnosis Motivation Institute (HMI) in Tarzana, CA, pioneered some excellent work in this area, which he referred to as Physical and Emotional Suggestibility (how we learn and communicate), along with Physical and Emotional Sexuality (how we behave). For more about Dr. Kappas' E&P models, check out the videos presented by the HMI at:

http://www.hypnosis.edu/streaming/ep/.

Laws Governing Suggestibility

There are 5 natural laws governing suggestibility:

1. The Law of Reverse Reaction (also known as "Reverse Psychology")
2. The Law of Repetition
3. The Law of Dominance
4. The Law of Delayed Action
5. The Law of Association

It's important to understand how and where these laws come into play when working with a client in hypnosis, because the proper utilization of these laws will greatly increase the success of the suggestions you use and the work that you do.

We are motivated by two emotions: pleasure and pain. The fear of pain can immobilize our ability to make rational decisions, so that any decision made for us is readily accepted, because it represents the path of least resistance. Similarly, our desire to gain pleasure can cause us to react without fully thinking through our decisions to see if they logically make sense.

The advertising and marketing industry capitalize on these two emotions very heavily to motivate us into parting with our hard earned money in exchange for their product or service, which promises to either help us avoid pain, or give us pleasure.

The *Law of Reverse Reaction* states that an individual will respond to the stronger part of a suggestion, if the alternative is presented as considerably weaker. For example "Your eyes are stuck shut. You can *try* to open them, but, the more you *try,* the harder they stick together." In this example the word "try" implies failure, a weaker suggestion to the command "stuck shut" so the applied law rejects the attempt to "try" and follows the command of "stuck shut".

The *Law of Repetition* is an easy one to understand, since it's the basic way we develop any new skill. When we first begin to learn something new we find it difficult or awkward but, over time, as we condition our minds and bodies through repetition, we get better and better at the new task, until it becomes an unconscious effort. By applying this law when working with our clients, we can compound the effectiveness of a suggestion by repeating it over and over again, while the subject is in a hypnotic state. This helps to develop new neuropathways and ingrain the suggestion as a newly developed habit.

The **Law of Dominance** can be described as a position of authority so that commands are taken in more readily. This can be accomplished by establishing strong rapport with the client and demonstrating your knowledge and skill, to create your position of authority in the hypnotic process.

The **Law of Delayed Action** states that a suggestion may not take effect immediately, when delivered in an indirect manner. In fact, it may not take effect until the situation that the suggestion is meant to overcome presents itself again to the client. For example, suggestions of increased confidence when speaking in front of an audience may not appear to be in effect until the client actually gets in front of an audience, at which time the suggestion kicks in and the client begins to feel confident.

The **Law of Association** is part of our learning modality, whereby we begin associating feelings or states to things that we develop an identification of. We can use this when working with clients, by creating new positive associations to events, thoughts or behaviors that once had negative associations, or vice versa in the case of aversion therapy.

Another application of the *Law of Association* states that if a client accepts the first suggestion, they will likely accept the second suggestion and so on. One way of accomplishing this is by creating what's known as a "yes set". Get the client to agree on a couple of obvious "truisms" before making your suggestion for change. When they agree to the truisms, then they are likely to agree with the suggestion. Sales people use this technique a lot, because it's human nature to find pleasure in saying "yes" and pain in saying "no". Once we fall into the pattern of saying "yes", then it's difficult to change gears and say "no".

Guiding People into Hypnosis

I say "guide" someone into hypnosis, because, that's all we can really do. You can't force someone to be hypnotized against their will; all you can do is help to guide them into hypnosis on "purpose" as opposed to by "accident", which is what normally happens to us without our even knowing it.

Getting someone into hypnosis is the easy part. What to do with them once they're in, that's where the skill comes in. However, since we need to guide them there first, let's cover the "How" and then we'll cover the "What."

The Hypnotic Contract

As we mentioned at the beginning, in the section on Myths and Misconceptions, you cannot be hypnotized against your will. In order for you to hypnotize your client you have to have established the right level of rapport and trust and you have to establish the "hypnotic contract."

The "Hypnotic Contract" is an agreement between you and your client, where they agree to be hypnotized and they agree to let you hypnotize them. This can be established very directly by just asking "Are you ready to be hypnotized?" If they agree, then ask "Do you want me to hypnotize you?" Again, if they agree, then you have established the "hypnotic contract."

This contract can be established indirectly as well. For example, when a stage hypnotist asks for volunteers to come on stage, the sheer act of going up on stage pre-supposes that the subject agrees to be hypnotized and agrees to allow the hypnotist to hypnotize them.

Traditional Inductions

Hypnotic inductions have evolved a lot since the early days; we've come a long way from swinging pocket watches. Following are some of the more widely used hypnotic inductions:

Progressive Relaxation

Most new hypnotists learn the progressive relaxation as their first hypnotic induction. It's easy to learn, it's hard to get wrong, and it's effective. The only downside is that it takes too long. The basic principle of the progressive relaxation induction is to ease the subject into hypnosis (basically bore the subconscious into submission).

You start off having the subject sit in a comfortable position, semi-recumbent is best, but not lying down (we don't want the subject to drift into sleep), then have the subject take some deep breaths and close their eyes. Then, progressively have the subject relax the muscles in their body either starting from the feet and working up toward the head, or starting from the head and working down toward the feet. An example of a progressive relaxation script can be found in Appendix C.

Arm Raise Induction

The arm raise induction is more sophisticated than the progressive relaxation induction and so it takes a higher level of skill. The reason it's more sophisticated is that you can use it to both induce hypnosis and test for suggestibility type.

Have the subject sit in a chair next to your desk (or a table), sideways to the desk with one arm sitting on top of the desk. Position the subjects arm so that when the hand is raised, it can easily touch their face. Have the subject stare at the wrist of the arm sitting on the table, then ask them if they can "visualize or imagine" their hand with their eyes closed.

We say "visualize" or "imagine" because not everyone processes information visually, so not everyone can create visual images in their minds (actually, everyone can, but some are not consciously aware that they are doing so), however, everyone can "imagine" so this allows us to cover all of our bases.

Now tell the client:

"Now, with your eyes closed, concentrate on your breathing. When you feel your breathing begin to change, nod your head yes". *[Whenever we focus on our breathing it will always change.]*

"Next focus on your eyes and relax the muscles around your eyes and eyelids, and when you feel the eyes trying to roll upward under your eyelids or a flickering of the eyes, then nod your head." *[When the eyes are closed, they tend to move around on their own.]*

"When you become aware of dryness in your lips and throat and a tendency to want to swallow, nod your head." *[This happens automatically, but when we suggest that it will happen and it does, it confuses the client and they believe that it's happening because of the induction. We ask the client to "nod" their head yes, instead of responding yes, because this creates additional overload. We have already taken away the sense of sight by having them close their eyes, now we're removing the ability to speak, which creates more overload.]*

"Now, imagine that I'm taking hold of your wrist and pulling it up. When you begin to feel some tension in your biceps or a lifting of your wrist, nod your head. Your hand will continue to rise in rhythm with each breath you take in. When you feel this, nod your head yes." *[Continue to suggest "lifting up" or "rising up", emphasizing the word "up" on the clients inhale. This is a very useful technique. When we inhale, our upper body tends it rise, giving a non-verbal suggestion of lifting and rising. Inversely, when we exhale, we tend to experience more of a sinking feeling, which can be useful as a deepening technique later on in the induction.]*

"When your hand touches your head, you will reach the peak of your suggestibility and will go deeper into the hypnotic state." *[This statement does two things, it pre-supposes that they are "already" in hypnosis and will only go deeper, second it's building up anticipatory anxiety that something is going to happen when their hand touches their face. They may or may not have any conscious awareness that their hand is actually moving, so when it finally does touch their face, it will be a little bit of a shock, which is just enough to send them over the edge and deep into hypnosis.]*

All of the physical changes mentioned in the preceding patter will occur naturally, but because we mention it and bring it to the client's awareness, it creates the perception that we are making it happen. It also builds the "yes" set, mentioned earlier in this book. Each time something happens, and we have the client confirm that it's happening; we get a "yes" as well as compliance to follow our instructions.

The way you use this induction to test for suggestibility is to change between making direct suggestions and indirect suggestions and observing which suggestions have the most effect.

Eye Fixation Induction

The Eye Fixation or Eye Fascination induction is a very common induction (the old "pocket watch" induction is a form of eye fascination induction). Eye Fixation can be accomplished in many ways, having the client stare at a spot on the wall, or a flickering candle, or a pen light, or a shiny coin, or just about anything that one can stare at, which doesn't change a lot (staring at the TV doesn't count, although it can have its own hypnotic effect). The key is to have the point of focus slightly above normal eye level, so that the client has to look up slightly. This causes fatigue in the eyes, which is the effect we are looking for.

When you see the client's eyes begin to fade, or water, or begin to blink more frequently, you can begin your patter. Begin to suggest rapidly and with a paternal voice, that the client's eyelids are growing heavier and heavier and will soon have a tendency to close. This will be true, because the fatigue in the eyes makes them feel heavy and tired. Continue this patter until you see the client's eyes begin to flutter. They will normally close on their own, but if they don't, you can suggest that when they feel the eyes are just too heavy, then just let them close and they typically will.

Once the eyes are closed, move your hand very rapidly to their forehead and touch them lightly on the forehead, while snapping your fingers with the other hand and saying "Deep Sleep!" Then follow up with a deepening technique.

The eye fixation induction is a great tool to use when working with children. Because they often lack strong skills of concentration, giving them something to look at helps them to stay focused.

Auto-Dual Method

Sometimes a client comes in that is highly analytical and will try to talk themselves out of hypnosis. They may have a fear of being controlled by the hypnotist and therefore resist standard inductions. The auto-dual method is a way of preventing these clients from over-analyzing your induction: by leading them to believe they are hypnotizing themselves, causing them to enter hypnosis through a form of misdirection.

Here's how it goes: Have the client sit in a straight-backed chair. Tell them to place their feet flat on the floor, and to place their right index finger on the pulse of their left wrist, and to stare directly at the fingernail of their right index finger. You have now gotten them to follow three suggestions (again creating a "yes" set and compliance to follow directions). Now have the client repeat after you:

"I will now enter the state of hypnosis for the purpose of deep relaxation and focused self-control. I will count from five down to zero, and with each count, I will become more and more deeply relaxed. When I reach zero, I will go deeply asleep. Five...I begin to feel my breathing growing deep, gentle and rhythmic." *[Suggest this just as their breathing begins to change]*.

"Four...I begin to feel heaviness in my eyelids, as I become drowsier and sleepier." *[The subject's eyes will naturally begin to tire from staring at their fingernail]* "Three...I begin to feel every muscle, nerve, and fi
er in my body relaxing...deeply relaxing. Two...My arms, my legs, my entire body, are now deeply relaxed. One...My eyelids grow even heavier, my breathing is more rhythmic. I am deeply relaxed. Zero...Deeply asleep!"

By having the subject repeat the words after you, you prevent them from analyzing what is being said; so, when you reach zero, they are psychologically and physically prepared to follow the final suggestion of deep sleep.

Rapid Inductions

Now we'll discuss some rapid inductions. What do we mean by "rapid" inductions? Well, rapid inductions are inductions that get a subject into hypnosis very quickly, usually within 5 minutes. Here are a few of my favorites.

The "Dave Elman" Induction

Dave Elman (originally David Kopelman) was a hypnotist in the early 1900s. He studied and practiced hypnosis most of his life, first as a vaudeville act and eventually as a clinical therapist. His attention to the three key principles of an effective induction (speed of induction, reliability of the method of induction and sufficient depth for commands to be reliably effective) led him to develop the induction that bears his name.

The Elman induction is beautiful in its simplicity while, at the same time, very sophisticated in technical complexity. The induction is loaded with tests for suggestibility and depth throughout. It is effective for individual hypnosis sessions as well as when working with groups. And it is my preferred induction whenever I'm working with a subject for the first time, for therapy, or when I'm working with any sized group.

There are many forms of this popular induction; in Appendix D you will find the one I tend to use the most.

Milton Erickson's "Handshake" Induction

Milton Erickson suffered from a neural-muscular disorder throughout most of his young life and, as a result of that, he was a frail man, without a lot of physical strength, especially in his handshake. He learned to take advantage of this so called "weakness" and use it to his benefit.

He would start by shaking a subject's hand. Normally at first, but then gradually loosen his grip. He would then initiate the "hypnotic touch", also known as an "ambiguous touch", by tentatively alternate touching the subject's hand, first with the thumb, followed by a drawing away of the little finger, then a faint touch of the middle finger and back to the thumb again.

This process would present just enough vague sensation to draw the attention of the subject. The subject's attention would be drawn to your thumb. You move your little finger, which draws the subject's attention to the little finger. You brush their hand with your middle finger, which again draws the subject's attention to that finger. You continue rotating this vague touch around, constantly distracting and shifting the subject's attention

With this process you establish a "waiting set", thereby arresting the subject's withdrawal from the handshake. Then you touch the underside of the subject's wrist, with a gentle upward push, and then, almost, but not quite, simultaneously, you touch the top of the wrist with a slight downward push. These two "non-verbal suggestions" conflict with each other, causing the subject's arm to go into catalepsy. Then, gently remove your hand while the subject remains somewhat frozen in fascination. By this time, the subject will be in trance and open to waking suggestion.

The "Non-Awareness" Set

The "non-awareness" set is very similar to the "handshake induction" in many ways. The principle of the "non-awareness" is based on distraction, whereby you constantly shift the subject's attention, and therefore their awareness, to areas on which they are not currently focused, or of which they are not aware.

This constant shifting of conscious awareness prevents the conscious mind from being able to analyze what's going on and creates enough of a distraction to allow for a bypass of the critical factor. After 2-3 shifts of awareness, the subject will be in a sufficient enough state of overload to allow the hypnotist to convert the subject into a formal state of hypnosis.

For an in-depth study of this technique, check out Igor Ledochowski's master class on the subject at:

http://www.hypnosismasterclass.com/NonAwarnessSet.

Instant Inductions

Instant inductions are hypnotic inductions that happen, well, instantly, or at least within a few seconds, usually less than a minute. All of the techniques outlined below are safe to perform with any subject, without any fear of injury or discomfort to the subject.

Now, you may run across videos of "amateur" or "ill trained" hypnotists performing some of the same techniques described below, but in a manner that is somewhat "violent" or "traumatic" to the subject. For instance, grabbing a subjects arm and then yanking them violently to the ground in order to "zap" the subject into hypnosis. This application of the shock induction is designed to highlight the hypnotist in a theatrical manner and takes irresponsible advantage of the subject, with little regard to the subject's safety. I believe that such displays, although theatrically awe-inspiring at the time of execution, have a long-term negative affect on the profession of hypnosis, and may create more anxiety in the eyes of the general public toward hypnosis, as opposed to creating a sense of confidence that their safety would be well cared for in the hands of the hypnotist.

All of the techniques described below can and should be performed with the subject's safety as the number one priority. None of the techniques require any "violent" or "traumatic" action, and can accomplish the required state and depth of hypnosis desired, in a safe and comfortable manner for the subject.

For a detailed explanation of Instant and Rapid Inductions, see my workshop DVDs on the subject. You'll get demonstrations of several techniques, along with a breakdown of the mechanics involved in each. For more details, visit my site at:

http://www.HypnotistMichaelWhite.com.

The Principles of an Instant Induction

Almost all instant inductions are a form of "shock" induction, where the subject is startled, creating a temporary bypass of the critical factor, usually only allowing enough time to get one command in..."Sleep!". Figure 2 shows what happens during an instant induction. 1. Shock the subject. We'll discuss several ways of doing this. 2. The clients mind has a "What the...?" moment, creating a temporary bypass of the critical factor. 3. You have a split second to get in a single command..."Sleep!" 4. The subject drops into deep hypnosis, even to the levels of somnambulism. 5. The subject quickly begins to recover. 6. The hypnotist must keep talking to hold the subject at depth.

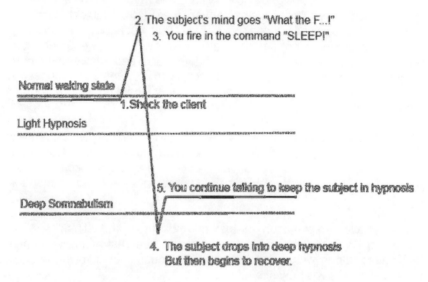

Figure 2: The Instant Induction Process

As I mentioned earlier, all instant inductions follow these same principles and steps to create a deep hypnotic state in their subjects instantly. It's important to keep in mind that a level of rapport should be established with the subject to achieve the most effectiveness with an instant induction.

The Eight Word Induction

"Push on my hand...close your eyes...SLEEP!"

That's it.

Here's how you do it. Hold your hand out in front of the subject, palm up. Have the subject place their hand, palm down, on top of your hand, then say to them "Push down on my hand." When they start pushing down, push up against them to create tension between you, and then say to them "Close your eyes." When they close their eyes, quickly remove your hand out from under their hand and say, in a commanding voice, "Sleep!"

Since they are pushing down on you, they are also pushing their weight forward. When you quickly remove your hand, they are temporarily lunged forward...this creates the shock we need for the "What the ....?" moment and the bypass of the critical factor. We quickly drop in the command for "sleep" and send the subject into somnambulism. Then we just follow up with our "deepener" (see below) of choice and begin working with the subject in hypnosis.

The "Arm Drop" Induction

This is a very easy instant induction, and very effective. It starts out like a handshake. The subject expects you to shake their hand up and down, but instead, you pull downward and in toward you, causing their shoulder to jerk forward slightly. Now, this is important. You don't have to pull their arm out of its socket, or throw them on to the ground; just a "slight" jerk of the shoulder is all that is needed to create the shock we need. Then we throw in our command for "sleep" and follow up with our deepener.

The "Butterfly" Induction

This is an interesting induction that's also fun to do. Have the subject sit in a chair. Hold your hand, fingers spread, in front of the client's face, slightly above eye level. Tell the subject to follow your fingers with their eyes and their head. Begin wiggling your fingers and moving your hand up and down and back and forth, ensuring that the subject is following your hand with their eyes and their head.

Once you get compliance, continue to wiggle your fingers and slowly start to lower your hand, drawing the subjects head forward and down toward their knees. This will also have a natural effect of causing their eyes to begin closing. When their head gets close to their knees, then snap your fingers and command "Sleep!" Follow up with your deepener.

Prior to using this induction, make sure your subject doesn't have any back problems.

The "Head Tilt" Induction

This is another easy, but effective, instant induction (actually, they're all pretty easy, once you understand the principles). You can do this induction with the subject sitting or standing (standing makes for a very impressive demo). If the subject is going to stand, then before doing the induction, say to the subject "At all times your legs will remain firm beneath you. You can sleep standing up." This waking suggestion will drop into the subject's subconscious as soon as they drop into hypnosis and they will be able to stand while in hypnosis.

Cup your non-dominant hand behind the subject's head, if you're right handed, your left hand goes behind the head, at the base of the skull. Hold your dominant hand in front of the client's face and ask them to take a deep breath. At the peak of their inhale, gently tap the back of the subjects head, moving it forward "slightly" and simultaneously command "Sleep!", catching the clients head in your hand, then follow up with a deepener. A slow head rotation at this point makes for a nice augmentation to your deepener.

Let me repeat; "gently" tap the back of the head, you don't have to rip the subject's head off to get the effect you want. Just a slight movement of the head will be enough of a disorienting effect to create the shock necessary for the induction to work.

Deepeners

Deepeners are techniques that follow the initial induction into hypnosis, in order to create a more profound "depth" of the hypnotic state. Just about anything can be used as a deepener, if presented in the right context, but I'll discuss some of the more popular or commonly used techniques.

For increased effectiveness, time your deepener with the subject's exhale. When we exhale, we create a natural "sinking" feeling in our body. This sinking feeling is a non-verbal suggestion of letting go, relaxing or going deeper. We can utilize this with our deepening technique to compound its effectiveness.

Counting

Counting is a very easy to understand and utilize approach to deepening. We count down to deepen. For example, "As I count backwards from 10 down to 1, allow each number I count and each breath you exhale to double the state of relaxation you feel right now and go deeper into hypnosis. 10...9...8...7...etc.", and we count up to "awaken" for example, "In a moment I will count you up from 1 to 5, when I reach the number 5, and not before, you will awaken, fully alert and in a non-suggestible state. 1...2...3...4...5 eyes open, wide awake."

You can count in any way that makes sense for your subject. Simply count numbers backward. Count the number of steps as you have the subject imagining going down a stairway, deeper into relaxation. Count the number of floors as they go down an elevator into deeper trance (make sure you're not working with a client that has claustrophobia or a general fear of elevators). Count the number of steps along a pathway into a relaxing image, like a garden or beach scene. The variety of approach and available options are limited only by your imagination.

Touch

Touch can be a very effective deepener. Gently rocking the subject back and forth, or gently rotating the head while giving the suggestion of "going deeper" and "letting go." Another approach might be to gently press down on the subjects shoulder, while they are exhaling, giving a non-verbal suggestion to sink deeper into trance, this can also be accompanied by some deepening patter, either counting or just suggesting that the subject go deeper or relax and let go.

The key principle to keep in mind about touch is to be conscious about your subjects comfort with touch. If the subject is uncomfortable with touch in a waking state, they may not react as desired in hypnosis. As with any close contact with a subject, be conscious about any chance of misunderstanding of touch in general, especially when working with a subject of the opposite sex.

Fractionation

To "fractionate" is to break up into smaller parts or divisions of a process. In hypnosis, we use fractionation as a deepener, by inducing trance, then partially awakening the subject, then dropping them back down again and continue to repeat the process of awaken, induce trance, awaken, induce trance, to increase the depth of trance each time.

Think about when your alarm clock goes off in the morning. You may very well wake up before your alarm even sounds. Even so, when the alarm goes off the first time, you feel somewhat awake, but decide you can sleep a little more, so you hit the "snooze" button. Then 9 minutes later (most alarm clock's snooze modes are 9 minutes long) the alarm goes off, this time you're more tired than you were the first time, but you decide you can sleep a little more, and you hit the snooze button again. 9 minutes later, the alarm goes off again and this time you're even more tired than when the first alarm went off. This is an example of fractionation. Each time you hit the snooze button, you drift back a little deeper, then a little more, each time you hit the button.

How was this discovered in hypnosis? Well, in the early days of hypnosis, they discovered that, after they hypnotized a subject, when they came back a month later, the subject went into trance more quickly and more deeply than the time before. So, they decided to bring them in earlier, like once a week, and again, each time the subject came in, they went into trance more quickly and more deeply than before. They kept shortening the period between trances until they discovered that they could put a subject into trance, take them out and then put them in again, multiple times in a single session and this would cause the subject to go increasingly deeper into trance with each re-induction into hypnosis.

So, how do you use fractionation as a deepener? Well, once you get your subject into hypnosis, using whatever induction you choose (progressive relaxation, rapid Elman induction or an instant induction, etc.), then follow up with the following fractionation patter:

"In a moment I will count to 3, and on the count of 3, and not beforehand, you will open your eyes. When I snap my fingers and say 'Sleep!', this will be your invitation to close your eyes and return to this blissful state of deep relaxation, only twice as deep as you are now."

"Ready? 1...2...3 eyes open, now 'Sleep!' [Snap your fingers and watch as the subject closes their eyes] even deeper now. And again 1...2...3 eyes open, now 'Sleep!' [Snap your fingers again and observe the subject going back in more quickly] "that's right, you're doing great. [This time, don't let them get fully eyes open before commanding sleep. This becomes a little bit of a pattern interrupt and will drop them faster and deeper] "One more time now and 1...2...3 eyes open, 'Sleep!'"

Now that you have fractionated the subject for depth, plant your post hypnotic suggestion for re-induction and continue on with the work with which you are helping your subject. A "post-hypnotic suggestion" is any suggestion you give to a subject, while in hypnosis, that you want them to keep with them after you bring them out again. For example, while the subject is in hypnosis, you might say "Each and every time I suggest sleep to you, for the purpose of hypnosis, with your permission; you will enter this state quickly and easily each and every time."

Signs of Trance

So you've learned a few inductions and deepeners and you have a subject to work with, but how do you know if your subject is actually in hypnosis? Well, there are several physiological changes that can occur during hypnosis, which can be clear signs that the subject is in trance.

As a subject is entering hypnosis, they may display or experience some or all of the following:

1. Increased blinking or fluttering of the eyes, leading to eye closure
2. Increased lacrimation or tearing in the eyes.
3. Increased dryness in the mouth and lips, or increased salivation and a tendency to swallow more often.
4. A change in breathing, either deeper diaphragm breathing or more rapid shallow breathing.
5. Increased relaxation of the facial muscles or relaxation of all major muscles (Relaxation is not a pre-requisite for hypnosis, but may occur naturally, once the subject enters the hypnotic state).
6. An increased tolerance for inconsistencies or anomalies in perception, logic or experience, known as "trance logic."
7. Increased "literalness" in the subject's responses.
8. A decreased ability or desire to respond verbally.
9. Feelings of warmth.
10. Feelings of heaviness or lightness.
11. Feelings of numbness or tingling in the extremities.
12. A feeling of floating.

There are other signs that may be observed from time to time but, in my experience, these are the most common.

Often times a subject will not realize the moment that they enter a hypnotic state and may even be convinced that they were not hypnotized at all, even though they show clear signs of trance and follow all of your suggestions. It's important to provide "convincers" to the subject, while they are in trance, as proof of trance when they are emerged.

Depths of Trance

There are several "depth" scales for hypnosis, some over 100 items long. For the sake of discussion here, I'll use the simplest scale. When we talk about "depth" of hypnosis, it's a bit misleading. The hypnotic state is more holistic, but referencing depth is a little easier to conceptualize; however, what we are really trying to achieve are levels of "intensity".

You see, we are always in a state of suggestibility; it's only the level of "intensity" that changes. If we were totally un-suggestible, we would have difficulty communicating with other people...we would have difficulty communicating with ourselves. The level of openness to suggestion determines the "intensity" of hypnosis. So by increasing the level of openness, we say we are creating "depth" in hypnosis. For now, we'll work with the common vocabulary and reference "depth" of hypnosis, knowing that in reality we are talking about "intensity" of hypnosis and suggestibility.

Here are the conceptual levels of depth of hypnosis (simplified format):

Level 1 – Light Trance – Relaxation, eye lock (catalepsy of the small muscles), access to emotional responses.

Level 2 – Light to Medium Trance – Catalepsy of the larger muscles (arm lock/rigidity).

Level 3 – Medium Trance – Affect olfactory (smell) and gustatory (taste) with suggestions. Block numbers (aphasia).

Level 4 – Medium to Deep Trance – Achieve analgesia (feeling of touch, but absence of pain).

Level 5 – Deep Trance – Positive Hallucinations (Seeing something that is not there).

Level 6 - Somnambulism – Negative Hallucination (Not seeing something that is there). Anesthesia (complete absence of feeling).

Stage hypnotists strive to reach levels 4-6 for some of the most impressive hypnotic phenomena. These levels are also the most ideal for working with clients in hypnotherapy, as these levels allow you to do age regressions, timeline therapy, revivification of memories and experience, and give your subject access to resources they may not otherwise have access to at a conscious level.

Testing for Depth

We mentioned some ways to test for depth in describing the levels of hypnosis. Eyelid catalepsy is an easy test for light trance and it's even built into the Elman induction. The Arm Rigidity convincer is a great test for medium depth; as a matter of fact, the deeper the trance, the larger the muscle group that can be affected by suggestion. Smaller muscles, like eyelids, for light trance; medium muscles, like arms, for medium trance; and larger muscles, like legs and torso, for deeper trance.

When testing for depth, you should use your observation skills to observe that the subject is complying with the suggestion before testing. For example, when giving suggestions that their eyes are locking shut, observe that they are actually clinching their eyes closed before asking them to test that the eyes are actually stuck.

Another example, when suggesting to the subject that their arm is becoming stiff and ridged like a steel bar, observe that the client's triceps muscles are actually flexing, indicating that the arm is locking, before having them test for the inability to bend the arm.

In both catalepsy tests, we are utilizing the Law of Reverse Effect in your patter giving a strong suggestion (your arm is locked tight like a steel bar), and a weaker suggestion (try to bend the arm, but find it remains locked tight). The stronger suggestion will be accepted and the weaker suggestion "try" will fail.

We call these tests "convincers" because when the subject can't open their eyes or bend their arm while in trance, then you can remind them of this phenomenon when you bring them out, so that they become "convinced" that they actually entered the hypnotic state. This conviction that hypnosis actually occurred will re-enforce the suggestions given and allow them to be more readily accepted by the subconscious.

Failure to do convincers for your subject could run the risk of undermining all your hard work while in trance. The reason is that most people are unaware when they slip from normal consciousness to the hypnotic state, because perceptively, there's no difference. They can still see, feel and hear everything that's going on, which may not be in alignment with what their expectation of the hypnotic state is.

Even when you tell a subject ahead of time that they will be able to hear everything, when you bring them out of hypnosis, especially if this is their first time to experience it, they will often say "I don't think it worked, I could still hear you." So, that's why the convincers, especially for first time inductees, are so important: because when their eyes get stuck, or they can't bend their arm, then there is no doubt to their conscious or subconscious mind that something "hypnotic" has occurred.

This new "knowledge" that they truly were hypnotized, re-enforces the suggestions they were given while in trance and allows those suggestions to penetrate even deeper. So do convincers whenever you can. If you don't do them, it doesn't mean that you will fail, but why not stack the deck in your (and your subjects') favor.

Hypnosis for Therapy

Ok, sure, hypnotizing people can be entertaining and great fun, but the real value of hypnosis is to help facilitate real positive change in people's lives. In this section we'll discuss using hypnosis as a therapeutic tool for the betterment of mankind.

Finding and Screening Clients

Finding clients is the biggest challenge for the new hypnotist. There's a temptation to work with friends and family, which is fine for getting volunteers to practice inductions and "light" work, like improving memory, or sleeping better, or increased confidence. However, when it comes to doing serious therapy, the old saying "You can't be a prophet in your own land" comes to mind.

Your friends and family know you as "you" not as a skilled professional hypnotist, so there may be some resistance in working with you on serious issues. The close relationship and history you have with them can cause some uneasiness in discussing deeply personal issues. Also, when you do hypnotherapy with someone, it affects the relationship you have with them in a way that can't be changed back. This isn't necessarily a bad thing, just something you need to be aware of. In general, it's best to work with people in whom you have no emotional investment.

By far, word of mouth is your best marketing tool. Do good work and the word will get around. Collect testimonials from your clients and post them in a binder in your waiting room (if you have an office) or on a web site. Other traditional marketing and advertising methods (papers, magazines, flyers, radio ads, etc.) are also effective, but are beyond the scope of this text. The key thing to remember is to track how people "hear" about you and funnel your marketing dollars in the direction of the methods that generate the most leads.

The First Meeting

Ok, so you get a lead, or better yet, a referral, and the prospect contacts you. Your first meeting is likely to be by phone. This probably goes without saying, but always be "upbeat" and "confident" on the phone. Be friendly and convey an intense desire to help, but not in a desperate tone. You want something good "for" them, not "from" them.

Get an overview of what the client wants help with. Most likely, what the prospect initially calls you about is not the thing they truly want to work on. Often, clients come in with "lesser" issues to "try you out" and see if you are the real thing. Once they become comfortable with you, they will begin opening up to you about the "real" issue.

Client Intake Form

The client intake form is a simple form to start a client record when receiving new clients. Basic information is gathered, like the client's name and contact information. A sample form can be found in Appendix A of this book. You should create files for your clients and keep this form, along with notes and recordings of each session you have with the client. That way, you can go back through your notes and recordings to keep the client's issues and progress fresh in your mind.

Client History

With the client history, you should gather information about the patient's past treatment of the issue in question. Have they been to another hypnotist? What was the outcome? Why are they changing to you? What type of induction was used in the last session? Are they aware of any anchors that were established? Etc.

If it's a medical referral, get information about who their primary care provider is. How do you contact the doctor, so that you can keep the doctor up-to-date on the client's progress? The client should understand that they have a "team" of people helping them with their issue and that team consists of you as their hypnotist, their doctor, themselves and any other support groups that may be involved (spouse, family, etc.).

In gathering the client's history, it's also important to gather information about how long they have had the presenting issue to be addressed. Have they tried to overcome it in the past? What method did they use? Was it effective and if so, for how long? What benefits do they receive from their current behavior (all habits have some hidden benefit, otherwise people wouldn't do them)? What indicators are they expecting to let them know that they have achieved their goal?

When to Get a Physician's Referral

Any time you believe that there could be a physiological cause to your client's issue; it's a good idea to get a Physician's referral. Any sort of treatment to deal with pain management should be preceded by a doctor's referral. When working with clients who desire (or need) to lose more than 25 pounds, you should get a doctor's referral. Also, dealing with any sort of deep emotional trauma, like rape, abuse, paranoia, etc. should be preceded by a referral from a licensed psychologist or psychiatrist.

The Hypnosis Session

The hypnosis session starts with your first conversation with a potential client. Your attitude about your ability to help the client with their issue, how you carry yourself with confidence, and the rapport you establish, are all key components to the initial session with your new client.

Preparing for Hypnosis

When preparing for the hypnotic session, make sure that your client is ready to do the work. Your client's attitude about hypnosis and its ability to solve their problem is crucial. Clients will often come in with fears and misconceptions about what hypnosis is and what you can use it for. You'll want to address these fears and misconceptions right off the bat, because your ability to do so (or not) will determine the success of your session with the client.

The Pre-Talk

The pre-talk is where you address any fears and misconceptions the client has about hypnosis. During this talk, you'll go over a discussion about what hypnosis is and how it works. You'll cover the model of the mind to educate the client on the conscious/subconscious communication process, explaining how we learn and communicate, as well as how will power is often undermined by previous experiences and knowns.

You'll discuss the client's problem with them, all the time letting them know that it's easy to work with and that it's something you deal with all the time (even if it's the first time you have encountered it). Their belief in your experience and skill will increase the level of effectiveness of the session and how easily their subconscious mind integrates the suggestions given.

Discuss the different types of suggestibility and, if it's your practice to do so, take them through any suggestibility tests and explain the results to them.

The Presenting Issue

After the pre-talk, it's time to discover more details about the client's "presenting" issue (what they have come in to work on) for example: to

48

stop smoking, or lose weight, or to overcome a fear of flying. Whatever it is, you give them a little bit of time to discuss the issue with you. For things like stopping smoking or losing weight you'll want to uncover some specific information, like, how long have they been smoking? What age were they when they started? Why did they start in the first place? Have they tried to quit before? If so, how did they quit? Was it effective? If yes, then for how long? What made them start back again? Etc. The more information you can gather the better.

This section serves two purposes. It's a venting process for the client, and it helps you and the client to gain some perspective around the issue, so that the two of you together, can come up with a plan to make positive changes.

The plan for positive change should consist of identifying the benefits that they believed they were getting from the habit (in the case of smoking, this could be relaxation, frequent breaks from work, etc.), and showing them how they can get the same benefits, and more, from other means without the need of the old behavior.

Then you want to develop a "success" image. What will it feel like when they are successful? How will they be treated by others? What will they feel about themselves? What will be the positive changes to their lifestyle and quality of living? This information will be used during the hypnosis session, in a technique called "future pacing" where you will have the client (in hypnosis) see themselves in the future, long after they have experienced the positive change they are working on, and seeing how their life has changed for the better. You will incorporate all of the "success" imagery that they outlined in this session, using their own words and descriptors, to create a sense of accomplishment.

Most of your work is actually done here in this pre-hypnosis session, because you are outlining the plan of what you will do, and building the foundation for success by creating the "proof" in the form of the "success" imagery.

The Work

Now you're ready to do the work. Take the client into hypnosis, using whatever method you are comfortable with. Deepen the subject and plant your post hypnotic suggestion for re-induction to be used in future sessions.

An example of a post hypnotic suggestion for re-induction is:

"Each time I suggest 'sleep' to you, for the purpose of hypnosis, with your permission, you will allow yourself to return to this state, or even deeper, each and every time, so that when we want to do hypnosis work together all I have to do is snap my fingers and say the word 'sleep' and your eyes will close, your physical body will relax, and you'll go in quickly and more deeply each and every time."

Now all you really need to do is re-iterate what you discussed in the previous step. The main difference is that now you at speaking directly to the client's subconscious mind, without interference from the critical factor.

You'll spend time reminding the client that the benefits they thought they were getting from the undesired habits are actually things they can continue to receive, but from more positive resources. You'll help the client develop the "success" imagery, either through visualization or imagination (if they stated before the session began that they have trouble visualizing) by getting as many of their senses involved as possible. You want to really get them into the feeling of experiencing the "success" state. Give them some suggestions for continually compounding the suggestion even after the session is over. For example:

"Over the next few days or weeks, you'll notice that the color 'red' is much brighter and more noticeable than ever before. The color 'red' will seem to jump out at you everywhere you look. It could be as small as a light on your computer, or as big as a billboard. It could be the brake lights on the car in front of you, or the stop lights on the street, but the color 'red' will be more vibrant and more noticeable than ever before. And each time you encounter the color 'red', it will re-enforce these suggestions and make them even stronger and allow them to sink even deeper into your subconscious, allowing you to create profound, positive changes in your life, even more quickly than you ever imagined."

Then begin the process of bringing your client back to normal consciousness.

The "Double Dip"

Here's another "DRT" (Dirty Rotten Trick). When you tell the client that you are about to bring them back out of hypnosis, at that point, they start to believe that the session is over, so whatever resistance they may still be holding on to, they will let go. So, when you begin to count them back up you'll say something like…

"And now, in a moment, I will begin counting up from 1 to 5, and at the count of 5, and not before, you will be fully awake, alert, feeling absolutely fantastic."

Then you say…

"And 1, always go a little bit deeper…"

This is sort of a verbal "shock" induction because they're thinking "I thought we were coming up but he just said go deeper." Then, and here's the DRT, you quickly repeat the suggestions you gave them for change and summarize what they can expect to happen as proof of the change. At this moment their guard is completely down, because they thought the session was over, so your suggestions will enter much deeper than before. Then you continue counting them up and out of Hypnosis.

Once you have counted them out, you hit them with the "double dip", and repeat the suggestions again, re-iterating to them how they will be successful. Now how is this double dipping? You counted them out already…right? Well, yes and no. You see, the truth is, that the average person can take anywhere from 5-15 minutes to fully emerge from a deep hypnotic state, so for those 5-15 minutes, they are still in a hyper state of suggestibility, so you give them what's known as a 'hypnotic blitz" to re-enforce the suggestions and the expected outcomes and finish off with a waking suggestion that they "feel fantastic" in every way.

Ending the Session

At this point, you are pretty much done with the session. Now you can talk about what you will do in the next or follow-up session, if it has been determined that additional sessions are needed, because you either ran out of time, or you're dealing with issues that require multiple sessions to work through, like weight loss for more than 25lbs.

You'll also want to ask for their testimonial and entice them to actually give you one, by offering them some sort of gift or discount on future sessions or something. Remember, testimonials are your best marketing tool. You might also talk to them about giving you referrals.

Dynamic Scripting

Throughout this book I have provided you with sample scripts and script segments that you can use to create boilerplates for your inductions and even some scripts for deepening and some minor work. However, I'm reluctant to provide you with detailed scripts for resolving specific issues. The reason is that many hypnotists starting out become dependent on scripts to do change work with their clients. It's tempting to start out this way, because it seems that the hard work has already been done by someone else and you can just re-use their technique to get the same results. The truth is that scripts written in a general way are a "shotgun" approach to therapy and won't be nearly as affective as a script customized for your client.

So, how do you "customize" a script for your client? Turns out, it's really easy. You see, we all respond best to our own "language" and I don't mean this in a cultural sense, strictly speaking. What I mean is that we each have a vocabulary that we use regularly to describe our reality. When our clients speak to us, they use this vocabulary to describe their issues. They also use this vocabulary to describe their desired outcome, as well as the "proof" that would prove to them that the change work was successful.

By identifying the key words they use in their descriptions of their problems, desires and proofs, we can use those key words to generate the perfect script for their presenting issue, on the fly. We do this by echoing back to our clients, while they are in hypnosis, the same words that they provided us prior to the induction. This is a very powerful technique and can create a very deep and powerful suggestion to the subconscious.

Ok, let me give you an example. Let's say that a client comes in with a fear of public speaking. You have them describe what they feel in relationship to getting prepared for a speech; stepping on stage for a speech; and actually delivering a speech. Even if they haven't made it through all of these steps, they still have some image or perception of what might happen and how they would feel about it.

Then we have them describe to us their desired outcome. They may describe themselves as feeling "confident" and "calm" while delivering the speech; how the words would "flow smoothly" and "effortlessly" from their mouths. We make note of these "desired outcome" key words and then ask them to describe how they would know that they were successful. They might describe how people would be "attentive" and "interactive" with their presentation, asking questions and participating in the dialog. They might describe the "praise" and "compliments" they would receive after the speech for doing such a great job. We also make note of these "proof" key words.

We take our client into hypnosis and get them into a calm, relaxed state. Then we walk them through some dynamic mental imagery or guided visualization to see themselves going through each of the steps to prepare for and deliver a speech, the whole time feeling calm and relaxed. Then we "pepper in" their "desired outcome" words to ensure that their "language" and "vocabulary" are used to strengthen the visualization. We follow up with visualization of the "afterglow" of their presentation, also using their "proof words" in the imagery, the whole time reinforcing and strengthening the feelings of "confidence" and "self-esteem".

Hopefully, you can see how using this approach gives you the resources you need to work with clients on nearly any issue, and generate a customized session that is worded perfectly for your clients subconscious, without having to rely on generalized scripts.

Changing Habits

Hypnosis is the ideal tool for changing habits. The reason for this is simple. Habits are developed in the subconscious mind through association and repetition. Neural pathways for a behavior are created and re-enforced over time, creating a habitual behavior.

As hypnotists, we can use this same powerful tool, our client's subconscious mind, to change old behaviors and establish new ones; only we can accomplish this in a manner of minutes instead of weeks or years.

One of the benefits we have in using hypnosis is that the subconscious mind has no awareness or true concept of "time" as a linear process. Our minds can jump from the present, into the past, back to the present and even forward to a perceived future. Because the mind is not restricted by the limitations of "linear time" we can accelerate the process of learning and thereby the creation of new neural pathways and habits in a much shorter timeframe than the conscious mind.

Fears and Phobias - What's The Difference?

So, what's the difference between a "fear" and a "phobia"? Well, both are anxiety states we feel in certain situations. The difference is that a "fear" has a known cause and a "phobia" does not. For example, if we get bitten by a dog when we are a child, we may grow up with a "fear" of dogs. We know this is a fear, because we know where the root cause of the anxiety comes from. On the other hand, take a "fear" of flying. If the person experiencing this anxiety was actually in, or almost in, a plane crash or other airplane related accident, then it's truly a "fear". Otherwise, it's a "phobia".

So, how does a "phobia" form? There could be several causes. Let's say you are running late for a flight and you don't have time to stop and eat. So you get on the plane with low blood sugar. Then your body starts to react to the low blood sugar. You start shaking, you develop some disorientation or anxiety and you try to figure out where these feelings are coming from.

54

With no understanding of the physiological cause of this state you may mistakenly associate these feelings to being in the airplane. If this happens a couple more times (you're late; you don't eat; you feel anxious when you get on a plane), pretty soon, just the act of getting on the plane is enough to trigger the anxiety state and now you have a "phobia" and unnatural "fear of flying" with no known root cause.

Working with Fears

When working with a fear, it's important to get as close as you can to the initial sensitizing event. When did the client first experience these anxiety feelings associated with whatever the fear is? The reason this is important is because "fears" are typically developed in our early years, usually under the age of 10, although they may not manifest themselves as fears until later on in life.

Following are some discussions on how these "initial sensitizing" events can be uncovered, and then how to use them to work with the client to overcome their fear.

Regression Therapy

Regression Therapy is a technique that takes advantage of the subconscious mind's inability to perceive "linear time" and allows the hypnotist, once the client is in hypnosis, to regress the client to earlier experience in their stored memories to uncover the initial sensitizing event.

Regressions can manifest themselves as "re-vivifications" which are vivid memories in surprisingly intricate detail, but still somewhat dissociated from the client. With a "full regressive state", the client actually steps into the experience as if they are experiencing it for the first time. They may act as if they are 5 years old again and will be able to describe smells, sounds, colors, and temperatures, all in great detail.

Now, some schools will teach never to use regression therapy, because of the fear of triggering what's known as an "abreaction". An abreaction is an intense emotional response that can manifest itself while a client is in hypnosis and encounters a very traumatic memory. Now, some emotional release during hypnosis can be expected and is usually desired, since the emotional release is good for resolving whatever issue the client is working on. These "minor" releases, the client crying or expressing mild to medium emotional response, are NOT abreactions. If a client has a true "abreaction" you'll know it. It will be very distinguishable from the other emotional releases.

There are key things to remember if you encounter an abreaction with your clients:

1. **Don't panic.** If you panic, the client will sense it and the situation will get worse.
2. **Don't touch.** Don't touch the client, because you could inadvertently create an "anchor" and then the next time someone touches them in the same way, they may re-experience the abreaction again, even if they aren't in hypnosis at that time.
3. **Tell the client "The scene fades".** Give the client some guidance out of the experience. Tell them over and over again that the scene is fading and that they are returning to a place of safety. Watch for signs that the client is calming down.
4. **Feel the chair, know they're safe.** Have the client re-orient themselves to the chair they are sitting in. This brings them back to the present and gives them some assurance that they are safe and no longer in danger.
5. **End the session.** Once you observe that the client is calm and fully oriented back to the present, then end the session and don't mention anything about what just happened. Chances are the client won't have any memory of what they experience, because the subconscious mind usually blocks these memories from conscious awareness, so if you tell the client what happened, they may re-experience a memory that they are not yet ready to deal with. If they pressure you for more information, simply tell them that there seems to be something that their subconscious mind wants to work on, and when they are ready, you will work with them on the issue. Do not deal with it in that session; schedule another session specifically to deal with that issue. That way, both you and the client will be in the right state of mind and be fully prepared to deal with the situation properly.

If you keep these safety measures in mind, the abreactions are not something to fear; in fact they can be a very helpful therapeutic tool when triggered in a controlled session. But heed this word of caution: do not engage in regressions with your clients until you have gained enough training and experience to be able to deal with the eventualities responsibly and confidently.

With all that being said, how do you go about performing a regression with your client? The process is actually very simple to accomplish. First, get your client into hypnosis and deepen them to the depth of somnambulism. Have the client experience the feelings associated with the fear they want to overcome. Really get their feelings to manifest very strongly, even giving them suggestions to intensify the feelings. When you observe that the client is truly experiencing the feelings intensely, by watching their physical and emotional reactions, then say to them:

"At the count of 3, go to an earlier time where you felt these feelings. 1, 2, 3 be there now."

Then, orient the client to the scene:

"First impression: daytime or nighttime? Indoors or out? Alone or with someone? How old are you? Describe what you see."

Make notes of the client's responses to these questions, because you'll refer back to this information during the re-integration phase of the therapy. Once you have all the information you need about this memory then regress them again. Ask them

"Is this feeling familiar, like 'Oh no, here we go again' or new, like 'what's going on here?'?"

Check their response. If it's familiar you know that you're not at the initial sensitizing event, so you have to regress further. If they say it's new, still test again to see if you can find an earlier time. Get them engaged in the feelings again...intensify them and go through the regression sequence again.

"At the count of 3, go to the earliest time when you felt these feelings. 1, 2, 3 be there now. First impression: daytime or nighttime? Indoors or out? Alone or with someone? How old are you? Describe what you see. Is this feeling familiar, like 'Oh no, here we go again' or new like 'what's going on here?'?""

You'll know you have reached the initial sensitizing event when you ask the client to bounce back to an earlier time and they keep coming back to the memory they're currently in. Now you can utilize "Informed Adult" or "Circle Therapy" to work through the issue.

Informed Adult

With the "Informed Adult" technique you basically build on the adage "If I only knew then what I know now", and utilize the wisdom they have as an adult to talk to their younger self (that is, to their subconscious projection of their younger self) to talk them through this scary experience, but with the knowledge that they will survive and that the adult will be there with them every step of the way.

You have the "adult" observe the "child" going through the experience and then have the "adult" coach and guide the "child" through the experience, only now with the knowledge that they will live through it and that the "adult" is there to protect them. Then have the "adult" give the "child" words of encouragement to build up their self-esteem and give them the resources and strength to go through the situation without fear.

Re-integration

Now have the "adult" give the "child" a big hug and bring the "child" into them, telling the "child" all along that they will be protected. Then have the "adult" watch the "child" grow up inside them, going through the various subsequent experiences, related to the fear, only now with these new resources and knowledge, living through each experience with their newly developed confidence and strength, all the way until the "child" becomes the "adult" in the current time.

Future Pacing

Future Pacing is where you take a client into a future time and situation to experience something that has not yet occurred, but would be the type of situation that might trigger a fear response.

Once the "child" is fully re-integrated into the "adult", you have your client visualize or imagine a situation in the near or distant future; when in the past they might have experienced fear, but can now go through the experience with a calm confidence. While doing this future pacing with the client, observe whether there are still any remaining anxieties in the situations described. If not, then your work is done; if there are, then you may be dealing with stacked anchors and so you start the whole process over again with the newly identified feelings.

Circle Therapy

Once you uncover the initial sensitizing event, circle therapy can be a great tool for collapsing the anchor (anchors occur when emotional responses become associated to events or memories and can be triggered by similar events and memories in the future).

The basic premise is this: while you have the client in the experience, ask the "adult" about a time before the event where the "child" was safe, then take them there and have them describe the situation. Then ask the "adult" about a time after the event when the "child" was safe. Take them to the time afterwards and have them describe the situation.

Now you have a safety point before the event, then the event, and then a safety point after the event. You have the "adult" enter the "before" safety point as the "child", then you have the "adult" inform the "child" about what is going to occur in the near future, but that they will survive it and will end up on the other side of the event in a safe place. Then take the "child" through the event and to the "after" safety point and have the "adult" praise the "child" for being so brave and strong.

Now, you just start looping (circling) through the events, starting at safety, through the event and ending back at safety. You loop several times, faster each time, having the "adult" inform the "child", watching the "child" go through and then praising the "child" and then back again. You do this several times and you'll observe that each time they go through the cycles; the emotional response gets less each time. This is the anchor collapsing in on itself so that the feelings of safety on both ends override the feelings experienced in the event itself.

Working with Phobias

When working with a phobia, there is no initial sensitizing event, only the feelings associated with the current event, so the approach is different than working with a fear and ultimately easier to work with. The recommended process for working with phobias is to do a "Progressive Desensitization" to change emotions associated with the event.

Progressive Desensitization

"Progressive Desensitization" is where you take the client into hypnosis and then slowly take them through the series of events leading up to and then through the event that causes them anxiety, all the while having them maintain feelings of calm and confidence.

So, here's how you do it. Take the client into hypnosis and deepen them. You don't have to deepen them too much, only to the point where you can produce a sustainable state of calm and confidence. You'll want to get these feelings as strong as you can.

Once you get the client to the proper depth and build up feelings of calm and confidence, then you slowly take them through the processes that lead up to the anxiety trigger. For example, if someone has a (phobia) fear of flying, you might have them imagine packing their bags, feeling calm and confident; then getting into the transport to take them to the airport, feeling calm and confident; then checking in at the terminal, feeling calm and confident; then getting on to the plane, feeling calm and confident; then experiencing the takeoff, feeling calm and confident; then getting through the flight and landing at their destination, feeling calm and confident; then getting off the plane feeling calm and confident.

You build on the fact that two opposing emotions cannot co-exist. They can't be calm and confident, and scared at the same time, and the more positive emotions will overrule the negative ones. So while you continue to sustain and re-enforce the feelings of calm and confidence, they won't be able to experience the fear. So, once their subconscious mind can experience the trigger event while experiencing calm and confidence, it will collapse the old association of fear and instill the new associations of calm and confidence.

Now, depending on the level of intensity of the anxiety associated with the event, you may need to run through this process a few times, until you can observe the client going through the event and feeling calm and confident. Then do some future pacing with them, imagining other situations which, in the past would have triggered the anxiety, and observe that they can go through those situations now, with feelings of calm and confidence.

As stated before, regression therapy and even circle therapy are advanced techniques, so get really good and confident with the "lighter" stuff, before venturing into dealing with people's fears and phobias. Get additional training and certification in these areas before working with real clients. Overall, use common sense when working with clients using hypnosis. Above all else, always keep the client's safety and comfort your top priority.

In the next couple of chapters we'll discuss how you can use hypnosis for fun and profit and in ways that will help to promote your practice and drive business and referrals your way.

Practicum

In the following few chapters I will cover some practical applications of hypnosis that you can use to get your hypnosis career off of the ground in a profitable way. The two primary drivers for people to seek out a hypnotist are to stop smoking or lose weight, so I will cover each of these types of clients in detail. Another driver is increased performance in sports, so I'll outline an approach to that field as well. With these three processes, you should be able to begin seeing clients immediately and begin building up your experience, as well as your name recognition.

Hypnosis for Smoking Cessation

Hypnosis is the best way to help the habitual smoker to quit. Why? Because hypnosis is the ideal tool to help individuals change their behavior patterns. While there are many products on the market to help address the chemical addition to nicotine, few, if any, of those products address the behavior patterns associated to smoking, or the emotional and psychological gains that smokers perceive they are getting from smoking.

The thing to keep in mind when working with smokers is that they have an internal conflict. You see smokers want to quit smoking, and smokers also want to keep smoking. They are conflicted, and this internal conflict is what sabotages their conscious efforts to quit.

Most people start smoking because of social influence and pressure from their peers who smoke, usually at a very young age, when they are most impressionable and lacking in self-esteem or will power. They continue to smoke throughout their lives, out of habit, and begin to develop positive associations to the act of smoking.

Ask most smokers and they'll tell you that they smoke to relax, or they smoke to curb their appetite, or they smoke because it gives them a chance to "get away" for a little bit and take a break from work. Most of these "perceived" benefits are coping mechanisms, so if you can teach a smoker how they can get the same benefits they "thought" they were getting from smoking, but from healthier options, then the smoking loses much of its appeal and power.

Where Does It Start?

Your session with a smoker starts with the very first contact. Whether that's your web site, marketing materials, or a phone call to your practice. They need to feel confident that you know what you're doing and that you have their best interest in mind.

Start with a pre-session interview. Find out why they want to quit: is it because someone asked them to, or because they decided on their own to do this for themselves? If they are doing it for someone else, it's unlikely to work, no matter what method they use. However, if they are truly compelled to quit then hypnosis can help.

63

You want to ask some basic questions to get some background information about the origin of their smoking: things they have tried in the past to quit; their motivations for smoking; and their motivations to quit smoking. In Appendix E you will find two sets of questions to help discover a person's motivations for smoking and for quitting smoking.

It could also be helpful to find out if they have ever tried hypnosis before. If so, what was their experience like? For how long did they quit? What sort of induction did the hypnotist use? This information can help you to adjust your session to fit their experience. You can include the techniques that they felt were effective and exclude those techniques that were less effective.

Structuring the Session

The session begins with the pre-talk and a series of reframes (changes of perspective). You'll begin by reframing fears and failures. If they have tried patches and gums, you inform them that these products only address the chemical addiction but do nothing to address the psychological, behavioral component of smoking. If they have tried to quit using will power, you can explain to them about the 88% working against the 12%. Explain how you will speak directly to their subconscious to help overcome their past negative behaviors and open up access to the resources they need to be successful.

Address their fears about failure, weight gain and withdrawal symptoms. Explain that the reason people typically gain weight when they stop smoking is because they replace cigarettes with food, however this program will give them other resources for coping with stress and anxiety, without the need for cigarettes or the need to replace cigarettes with food. Explain that they won't be losing anything, because you will show them how to get the same benefits that they thought they were getting from cigarettes, but from healthier sources, so they won't even notice the pangs, or may not experience them at all.

Symbolic Associations

Another thing you'll need to get from your client is any symbolic associations they have to smoking. This will be a little more difficult to drag out of them, but it's important to understand, because it speaks toward motivation to smoke.

You'll want to see if smoking plays a part in their self-identity. Do they identify themselves as a smoker? Do they smoke because it makes them feel cool, or rebellious, or independent? This is an indication that they have some internal image about what smoking represents and they are internally driven to try and live up to this image, which can undermine their desire to quit. Look for imagery, like the "Marlboro Man" or symbols of "masculinity" or "being sexy".

The Right Mental Attitude

Now, you'll want to find out if they "really want" to stop smoking. How motivated are they? Never "beg" your clients to quit, make them do all the work to find their own internal motivations for stopping.

Start off by "gently" asking them "Why do you want to quit?" The three main reasons people give are Family, Health and Money. Other reason could be negative social image, tired of being a slave to paper and tobacco, or some recent shock, which made them re-evaluate their habit, like someone close to them dying of cancer.

Now test their motivation by asking "Are you absolutely sure you really want to quit now?!" There are only three possible reactions to this question:

1. "Yes!" – They are enthusiastic about the idea of stopping. This reaction means that you are ready to begin your session.
2. "Yeah...sure." – They are on the fence. "Fire Them" until they are "really" ready to quit.
3. "I don't think so" – Again, "Fire Them" until they are "really" ready to quit.

Bottom line, if you get any reaction other than total enthusiasm, send them away to really think about it and to only come back when they are "really" ready to quit. If you want, you can offer to take them through a special "motivation to quit" session to help them with their decision. I would recommend charging them for this session.

When you first start out you may feel compelled to give sessions like these away for free. However, it has been my experience that "nothing ventured, nothing gained" so if they don't have an investment of some sort, then it will be less effective for them.

Motivation to Quit Session

This is the session you would take a client through if they are unsure whether they want to quit, and want your help to decide. You will use this session to really increase their motivation to quit, by getting them to really "feel" the consequences of a life as a smoker, as opposed to the life as a non-smoker.

Explain to your client what you are going to do and that the secret of this session is to help them to really get in touch with the "feelings" and "mental imagery" associated to smoking and not smoking.

Now, induce trance and deepen. Create two paths that lead to the future, the left path leads to a future where they continue to smoke. The "right" path leads to a future of non-smoking. Take them down the left path first and really build up the worst possible scenarios that could arise from a life of continued smoking – a horrible death, a destitute family, business failure, etc. Really build up and enhance the feelings in this visualization. Get them to describe their experiences and feelings along the way.

Now take them down the "right" path of becoming a permanent non-smoker. In this guided visualization, life is grand, the best of everything comes true, health, business, family, etc. Again, have them "really" experience the feelings of happiness, health and prosperity. Throw in as many positive emotions and scenarios as possible.

Now, bring them back to the present and integrate the lessons learned from both paths, really emphasizing the difference between both paths. Now ask them which path they want. If they are still undecided, then run through the scenarios again, building up the experience even more. If they choose the "right" path, then test them with the question "Are you really ready to walk down the path of a non-smoker, and be sure that this is the right path for you?" Some will decide on the spot, others will want more time to think it over, in either case, end the trance and let them decide or go off and think about it.

If they have decided to quit, then schedule a follow-up appointment to be their "stop smoking" session.

The Stop Smoking Session

While you are just starting out, give yourself plenty of time for this session, at least an hour to an hour and a half. Let the client know that after this session, absolutely no more smoking...period. We say this, and you can explain this to the client, because some people won't believe how easy it is to quit with hypnosis, and they think about testing themselves, by smoking just one cigarette. This is a huge mistake, because the old neuropathways are still there, and testing themselves in this manner will undermine all they have worked so hard to accomplish.

Now, induce trance and deepen. A moderate depth is sufficient. Utilizing the Dynamic Scripting framework presented earlier in this book, you can now go through a series of reframes while they are in trance. Talk about how they have smoked for "x" number of years and that they have had their fair share of cigarettes...they have not been cheated. Talk about how their subconscious mind has had its reasons for keeping this habit alive, but now they know that smoking is no longer what is good for them and that it's time to let it go.

Reframe the fact that all of the benefits that they once "thought" they were getting from smoking (confidence, relaxation, etc.), were not from smoking at all, but were from resources that have been inside them all along. At this point increase the feelings of relaxation and confidence and give them a trigger to revive these feelings whenever they need them. Tell them, "Each and every time you find yourself in a situation, which in the past may have caused you stress or anxiety, all you have to do is pinch your index finger and thumb together, then take a really deep breath, and as you exhale, release your fingers and say to yourself 'relax' and feel the relaxation wash over your entire body, from the top of your head, down to the tips of your toes."

Let them know that this is their tool to use anytime they need it, as often as they want, and that each and every time they use it, the effects get strong and stronger, each and every time.

Future Pacing

Now, take your client on a little journey. Have them visualize or imagine sometime in the near future, in a situation that, in the past, they may have been tempted to smoke. Have them see themselves now going through this situation as a non-smoker, feeling relaxed, calm and confident, totally unaffected by the scene. Do this with several of the situations, that they had told you in the initial meeting were common times or situations where they smoked. Run through each scenario, feeling relaxed, calm and confident and completely smoke free.

This future pacing technique builds up a feeling of accomplishment, and gives them a glimpse of a positive future, as if it has already happen. This helps to overcome some of the fear of the unknown, or uncertainties about what the future holds for them and will help to further integrate the suggestions into their new reality.

Test, Test, Test!

While you still have them in trance, test their conviction to quit. If the suggestions are going to break down, it's better to have them break down in front of you, so you can deal with them right away.

Have your client imagine smoking a cigarette and see what happens. If they are sickened by the idea, then reinforce these feelings of repulsion. If they say they enjoyed it, then you know that you still have a little more work to do. Have them describe the situation to you in great detail. What are they doing? Where are they? Are they alone or with someone? How does it make them feel? What is their perception of the scenario?

We're looking for clues as to the internal or external motivators that are still driving them, so that we can address those drivers specifically and dis-empower them, so that they don't become an issue when your client leaves your office.

Creating New Behaviors

Once you feel that the suggestions have taken strong effect within your client, you will want to help them to create new positive behaviors to replace the old ones that accompanied their smoking. Go back through the list of times and places that they used to smoke and have them describe to you their thoughts on healthier, more creative ways to deal with those situations, without smoking.

This exercise forces their subconscious mind to get involved in the process and creatively design new positive behaviors for your client, which will then be internal suggestions and motivations that will help them to stay on track.

Dealing with Saboteurs

The last thing to do while your client is still in trance is to teach them how to deal with saboteurs, such as other smokers, stress, curiosity, arrogance, etc. It's not uncommon for other smokers to undermine the success of someone trying to quit. They don't do this maliciously, or even consciously.

People are generally resistant to change, and if you change, it means that, in some small way, they too must change, so they will try to keep things the same as they have been. They may say things like, "come on, hypnosis? Man, you have tried to quit dozens of times in the past and you always start smoking again, so why bother, just accept the fact that you're a smoker and deal with it."

These types of comments may come from other smokers, or from non-smokers that have associated your client's identity with being a smoker, and so they are unwilling to change that perception, so they try to undermine your client's progress. Let your client know that these situations will come up, but they will be able to maintain their resolve and get through these situations, calmly and confidently.

Explain that they may feel cocky or arrogant that they were able to quit so easily and might be tempted to 'test' themselves. Let them know that this is unnecessary, and that they should be happy with the results they are getting and that the mere idea of "testing" themselves is nonsense and a ridiculous notion.

End the Session

Now, bring your client out of trance and use the 'double dip' technique described earlier in this book to reinforce the suggestions of calm, relaxed confidence and that they are on the "right" path toward a brand new future as a permanent non-smoker.

Hypnosis for Weight Loss

The first thing I need to say here is that if a client comes to you because they want to lose weight, and it's obvious that they need to lose more than 25 pounds, then you need to ask them to get a doctor's referral before you can work with them. The reason is that there could be a medical cause for why they are overweight, like a problem with their thyroid, and you don't want to accidentally do anything that could make that problem worse.

Three Classifications of Weight Gain

There are basically three classifications of weight gain. The first is neglect. We get caught up in our busy lives and we just stop paying attention to what we eat, and the amount of exercise we get. This is a common occurrence and the easiest weight gain to deal with.

The second classification is that food is used as a coping mechanism for stress, anxiety, depression, etc. This is also fairly common, and takes much more care to work with. Oftentimes you have to deal with the underlying traumas that trigger the need to eat, as well as doing some behavioral modifications to cope with the stress and anxiety.

The third classification is a physiological condition causing an imbalance in the body, like hyperthyroidism as mentioned earlier. This is why we always insist on a doctor's referral if the client needs to lose more than 25 pounds, so that if there is a physiological cause, then the doctor will find it and get them the appropriate medication. You can still work with these clients, but only after they have received a doctor's referral.

Negligence

Working with the first classification (those who simply neglect their bodies), is fairly straight forward: simply use the dynamic scripting method discussed earlier in the book to figure out their motivation and proof language, and provide them with customized suggestions to motivate them back into being more attentive to their health. Augment these suggestions with additional suggestions of increased confidence and self-esteem (we can never have too much self-esteem).

These individuals simply need a gentle, but positive, "nudge" to get them back on track again. This can usually be accomplished in a single session, with an occasional follow-up session. If they are competitive athletes, professional or amateur, then you may consider taking them through the Sports Hypnosis program outlined in the next chapter.

The Emotional Eater

The second classification, the "emotional" eater, will typically take a lot more work. They eat as a way to cope with life. They eat to celebrate; they eat to feel better; they eat because they are bored; they eat when they are stressed. This pattern of behavior is usually developed at a very young age and then reinforced over the years as they grow older.

Well-meaning parents and guardians contribute to this early stage of development, when food is used as a reward, or a bribe, or to occupy a child when the adult is too busy to pay attention to them. Here are some examples:

"You got good grades, let's go out to eat and celebrate!"
"Clean up your room and you can have some ice cream."
"I can't play with you right now. Here, have a cookie."
"I'm sorry you're feeling sad, here eat this, it will make you feel better."

It's clear to see how these individual actions, over time, can create patterns of using food as a means to change emotional states. Perhaps you have heard phrases like these said to you...maybe you have said them to a child in your life. There's no intentional malice here, however we must begin to understand that our actions and words form the belief systems and behavior patterns of our children, so we must be careful in what we say and do around them.

It has always been my philosophy and belief, that you can't tell your children not to "smoke and drink" while you have a beer and a cigarette in your hands. You must be congruent at all times in your messages to them.

Doing the Work

With emotional eaters, you often have to deal with the underlying issues that are triggering unwanted behavior. Then you have to help them to re-train their subconscious to access healthier resources to cope with these underlying issues. Help them to find other ways to deal with boredom, or stress, or anxiety, as well as healthier ways to celebrate the good things that happen in their lives, besides going out to eat.

Now don't get me wrong, there's nothing wrong with going out to eat as a celebration, just exercise some moderation. Also, I don't agree that people should deprive themselves of the foods they love, like cake or sweets. Deprivation breeds temptation. So have a piece of cake if you're hungry for it, just don't overdo it.

Changing Perspective

Teach your clients to change the way they look at food. Many of us are taught to "clean your plate", so when we are presented with a large plate of food, this pattern kicks in and we "must" finish it all. There are two approaches to working with this learned behavior. First, learn that it's ok to not finish all of the food on your plate. You can share some with another person, or save some for another meal. The second thing is to get smaller plates. Limiting portion sizes will allow you to manage your food intake more effectively, while still being able to fulfill this learned behavior of cleaning your plate.

Hypnosis for weight loss is rarely a single session, especially if you are working with emotional eaters. Let your client know that they have a "team" of people working with them to overcome these problems and that it will take some time. Their doctor is there to help them with any underlying medical issues, as well as advising on exercise and nutrition. You are there to help them develop better coping skills and to increase their motivation. And it's also important for them to understand that they didn't put the weight on overnight, so they should not expect it to "magically" come off overnight.

Know Your Limits

Some of the issues that come up when working with emotional eaters can be related to deep trauma, or repressed memories; so, before working with these clients, be sure you have the experience and training necessary to deal with whatever comes up.

Know your limits, and if you don't feel that you are ready or qualified to deal with these situations, then you should refer your client to another hypnotist. There's no shame or failure in doing so. We are there first and foremost for our client's well-being, and if that means that we must refer them out so that they get the help they need, then we have succeeded in helping them.

Hypnosis for Sports

Sports & Fitness is a 60 billion dollar industry. In addition to the world of professional sports, people all over the world take their sports and recreational time very seriously. Recreational time has become a place where people define themselves by the sport that they play.

Many athletes, professional and amateur alike, have discovered the power of augmenting their training with hypnosis. They do this to be developing anchored "triggers" to instantly access power states while training or competing.

There are a number of reasons why you would want to include working with athletes as part of your hypnotherapy practice, here are just a few:

- Great income potential: From sports teams, leagues and organizations to individuals
- Great clients
    o Clients already have:
        – An awareness of what they want to change
        – An understanding of what their issues are
        – Most likely, an ability to take direction
        – A strong desire to be willing participants
- Great satisfaction: Helping clients achieve success in a short period of time.

We can help athletes reach the "next level" of performance by helping them to identify and eliminate limiting self-talk. We can help them to overcome performance anxiety by addressing their fears and anxieties. Through customized sessions, we can help athletes hone their mental game for success and bring fun back into their practice and performance.

Here's an overview of the process:

A. Identify The Problem
   i.   What is adversely affecting the athlete or performer?
B. Identify Their Motivation
   i.   What are their beliefs, doubts & expectations?
   ii.   Is it Intrinsic or Extrinsic?
C. Change Their Perception of the Issue
   i.   Solutions
   ii.   The Mental Core

        a. Concentration Control
        b. Confidence Commitment
  iii.   Rituals & Practices
D. Apply Hypnosis
  i.   In State Learning
  ii.   In Vivo
  iii.   Monoideism

Identifying the Problem

When an athlete's performance starts to deteriorate, there are usually some problem signs. Following is a breakdown of some of the most common signs:

Problem Signs

- NO FUN: The athlete isn't having fun anymore – they're not playing with the same enjoyment they once had.
- MISPLACED FOCUS: They're focused on worries, doubts, anxieties and frustrations.
- DISTRACTED THINKING: Thinking too much causes hesitations, resulting in missed plays and errors, which leads to increased fears, diminished self-confidence and unmotivated play.

Where to Start

So, once we identify the problem where do we start to find solutions for our clients? Here is a suggested process to follow. Beginning with the first phone conversation and continuing with the first session, uncover the challenges your athlete is facing. By the second session, gain further insight into the root of their issue. LISTEN to what motivates them, and what their beliefs are and remember, let the client guide you. In subsequent sessions, as you further understand the problem, formulate their game plan for success.

Ask probing questions like:

- What age did you start?
- What level / division are you playing now?
- When did you first notice your performance issue?
- What is your long-term goal for this sport?
- What would you like to accomplish with hypnosis?

Identifying Their Motivation

We want to uncover what our client's motivations are. What we're trying to uncover here is whether their motivations are intrinsic (internal to themselves) or extrinsic (driven externally by others). We're going to ask questions designed to uncover this information, for example:

- What are their Beliefs?
  - Listen for "I'm too..." phrases.
- What are their Doubts?
  - You'll hear statements like, "I didn't practice enough...", or "I'm not..."
- Identify their Expectations?
  - Listen for, "I need to / I have to score" ...etc.
- Who tells them these things?
  - These "beliefs" have been brought in by external sources.

Understanding the Difference between Intrinsic and Extrinsic Motivators

Intrinsic Motivators are Internal and Task Oriented. Some examples are:

- Participation is pleasurable
- Effort is based on enjoyment of competition and excitement
- A desire to learn and improve for learning's sake
- Focus is on personal excellence
- Thrives on competition
- General exclusion of distractions

Why do Intrinsic Motivators work?

When an athlete is internally motivated they have greater stamina, rise farther in their sport, and have longevity. Advancement and success further perpetuates this positive momentum. They love what they do for its own sake, and they're more prone to stay focused on personal excellence and thrive on competition.

There are many payoffs to intrinsic motivators, including but not limited to: task-relevant focus; consistent levels of motivation; decreased stress; and elimination of distractions. These motivations can be carried over to other areas of their lives and provide a feeling of greater autonomy which increases their motivation. Helping the athlete find their fundamental goal is a key. Help them locate the inner meaning and enjoyment. Keep it fun. Keep it fresh.

How do Extrinsic Motivators Compare?

Extrinsic Motivators are externally oriented to things like trophies, scholarships, praise, large salaries, and fame. The education system puts a large emphasis on scholarships, trophies and medals. Society emphasizes salaries, or grants a seal of approval based on an athlete's skills, or income potential, often making these things the main focus.

Challenges to Extrinsic Motivation

When an athlete plays for themselves, no one else pulls the strings, and motivation comes from within. However, when extrinsic motivators are involved, athletes are more susceptible to losing their motivation. Externally motivated athletes are more likely to be distracted, and affected, by competitive conditions and situations. Fear of failure is characterized by high expectations, and results in a strong desire to "only" succeed.

Are Extrinsic Motivators ever helpful?

Extrinsic motivators can be helpful in circumstances where athletes lack inner drive for unpleasant modes of training. Mostly however, they yield short term solutions. It may help push an athlete to the next level, but the joy and appreciation of their success still has to come from within if the goal is to perform long-term.

More Examples of External Motivation

- Social approval or Social acceptance
  - What others think
  - Being embarrassed
  - Being scolded by parents / coach
  - Wasting hours of practice time
  - Not performing to others expectations
  - Focus on goals / tasks / personal achievements

Push toward Self-Motivation

Develop an internal drive or motivation based on a love of sports and let the athlete set the goals. Self-motivation is best; a long career is achieved from the love of sports.

Changing Perceptions

Perception is very important in Sports Enhancement. Hypnotherapists can change anxiety into confidence, boredom into motivation, misplaced focus to proper focus.

ANXIETY -> CONFIDENCE
- When the mind's perception of an experience exceeds its physical ability you have anxiety
  - When an athlete faces a new opponent they've heard is very good, they may experience nerves, self-doubt, and other physiological symptoms that can impede their ability to perform optimally
- When the mind's perception of an experience is one that's attainable, you have confidence
  - When an athlete performs a routine they've practiced many times, they're sure of themselves and are able to step out with confidence, get into the "zone" and achieve success

BOREDOM -> MOTIVATION
- When the mind's perception of an experience isn't challenging, the physical body gets complacent, resulting in boredom
  - They are not challenged by their peers and must be moved to a higher level in order to continue to achieve success

MISPLACED FOCUS -> PROPER FOCUS
- When the mind's focus is misplaced, redirect the focus to the game
  - When an athlete is angered by another player and focuses on revenge.
  - When an athlete is distracted by the audience or other players, it keeps their focus away from the game.

Changing Perceptions: Solutions

How do we solve these issues? How do you change an athlete's perception?

- Build Self-Confidence
- Remove Mental Blocks / Mental obstacles to success
  - Mental Rehearsal – anchor in new knowns
- Improve Focus - Focus on what is important and let everything else go
- Address the Power of Intention
- Address the Power of Expectation
- Remove Hesitations
- Mental Traps: Teach them how to recognize and avoid them.
  - Change negative self-talk and block out negative suggestions from others (See Rejection Proof Script)
  - Identify self-sabotage. Where do they not feel worthy to move forward?
- Shift from Extrinsic to Intrinsic motivation, if necessary
  - Identify their Beliefs – often brought on externally, not always positive.
- Change these beliefs, and you can change the outcome of their performance
- Motivation can have a snowball effect – it can keep growing and propelling an athlete to the next level and to higher levels of success
  - Pinpoint their Doubts
  - Uncover their Expectations
  - Remember the MENTAL CORE
- Repetition – The mind needs repetition.

Changing Perceptions: The Mental Core

CONFIDENCE * CONCENTRATION * CONTROL * COMMITMENT

These four qualities are the main mental qualities that are important for a successful performance. They are perfect examples of Intrinsic Motivators

CONCENTRATION – The ability to maintain focus

CONFIDENCE – The belief in one's abilities

CONTROL – The ability to maintain emotional control and focus regardless of distraction

COMMITMENT – The ability to continue working to agreed goals despite setbacks or losses

Changing Perceptions: Rituals & Practices

"Sports performance enhancement spills over into all aspects of an athlete's life."

Rituals and Practices helps to overcome issues, decrease anxiety and increase motivation.

Goal Setting

Not just a skill for performance, but a skill for life. Reviewing goals before an event or competition sets up the power of intention and the power of expectation.

Pre-Game Rituals

Pre-Game rituals can be as easy as narrowing focus, listening to rhythmic music, absorbing -themselves in film, anchoring the athlete to their equipment, or anything that the athlete does to prepare for practice or for a game.

Help your client to develop effective pre-game rituals by being the objective observer. Analyze their process to help them reach their objective. Work with your clients to identify or suggest rituals. Continually analyze what works and what doesn't. And modify or add to encourage success.

The Zone

This state is also known as a peak experience and, as discussed in an earlier chapter, it is one of the naturally occurring hypnotic states. Self-Hypnosis and Systematic Desensitization are effective for relieving anxiety and getting in "the zone."

Game Plan / Performance Plan

The Performance Plan brings together practical planning with mental preparation to ensure the athlete/performer is fully prepared to handle any situation that may realistically occur. It also gives them the confidence that comes from knowing they are well prepared, and helps to ensure they perform in a relaxed, positive and focused state of mind.

Help your athlete put together a *written* plan by helping them make a list of all the things they need to do: from starting to prepare for an event or game, all the way through to its conclusion.

Examples include:
- Preparing & checking equipment; repairing and/or replacing. "If you take care of your equipment, your equipment will take care of you."
- Making travel arrangements ahead of time.
- Packing equipment and luggage.
- Traveling to the site of the game or event.
- Setting up equipment.
- Waiting and preparing for the game or performance.
- Delivering the performance.

As this is a written plan, make sure it is in a form that is easy to refer to and to read. Have them keep it with them as they prepare for and play their game, or deliver their performance, referring to it whenever they need, either before or during the event. Focus on steps that help them feel successful.

Applying Hypnosis

"Hypnosis is where it all comes together."

Hypnosis is the "Mental Edge" every athlete is searching for. It helps to reinforce positive habits, resulting in: Hyper-awareness & More Focus

IN STATE LEARNING
- Technique used during hypnotherapy sessions.
- Encompasses relaxation.
- Allows your client to learn without fatigue.
- Helps them learn to be in the "flow" without being distracted by the crowd, the coach, their mental blocks, worries, doubts or fears.

IN VIVO

- A mental rehearsal technique.
- Used prior to an event to go through the motions, using visualization and mental imagery.
- Self-Hypnosis can be used "In Vivo" to reinforce goals.
- The word "In Vivo" is Latin for "within the living."

MONOIDEISM

- The ability to focus on ONE task at a time.
- Helps the athlete become conditioned to remain in a state of "fight" instead of "flight" when faced with stressors and distractions of the event.
- Monoideism IS hypnosis.
- Use this when closing in on the event.

General suggestions in Hypnosis

- Encourage change in fitness attitudes.
- Remove hesitations (i.e. choking, freezing, etc. during competition).

For a complete example of running a workshop, check out my "Sports Performance Enhancement Workshop" DVD at:

http://www.hypnotistmichaelwhite.com

Demonstrations

When you first start your hypnosis practice, it can take some time to develop a steady stream of clients, mainly because you are new and people don't know anything about you. One of the best and easiest ways to get your name out there is to do demonstrations. You can donate your time for free, or charge a nominal fee to speak at various functions. You can give talks about the power of the subconscious mind and the ability that people have to use their subconscious as a tool to help them achieve their goals.

During these talks, you can do group suggestibility tests to demonstrate the power of the subconscious, or better yet, you can ask for some volunteers (of course, picking out the ones that do the best during the group tests) to demonstrate an instant or rapid induction and then perform some simple hypnotic phenomenon, like eyelid or arm catalepsy, forgetting a name or number, or sticking someone's hand to a wall or table. Any of these are appropriate to do in these scenarios and make for an impressive display of your skills, as well as a convincer for the subject, and all those watching, of the power of hypnosis and the subconscious mind.

How do you get these speaking engagements? Well, there are many organizations out there that meet on a regular basis, and they are always in need of presenters and speakers. Examples of groups that meet frequently are the Rotary clubs, Elks Club and Toast Masters, just to name a few. The organizers of these meetings are always eager to find new speakers, especially if the speakers have an interesting topic and are economically priced, or better yet...FREE. And the best part is that the organizers often are in contact with the organizers of other groups and they share references and referrals for speakers.

These speaking engagements don't take a lot of time to prepare for, or to perform, and the marketing value is huge. You're bound to get several clients out of each talk, which has the potential to grow to even more with repeat business and referrals. So demonstrations should be a key component to your marketing and growth strategy.

Stage Hypnosis and Street Hypnosis

Many hypnotherapists frown on the profession of stage and street hypnosis, but the truth is that hypnosis may have been lost in obscurity if it weren't for the stage and street hypnotist. When the field of professional psychology trended away from the use of hypnosis in the 1800s, it nearly killed hypnosis as a therapeutic tool and may have been lost forever if it weren't for the band of street and stage hypnotists keeping the knowledge of hypnosis alive.

It wasn't until the early to mid-1900s that hypnosis began to gain notoriety again in the therapy circle, thanks to the work of Dr. Milton Erikson, David Elman and many others like them, who recognized the power that hypnosis offered as a tool for gaining positive and permanent change for their patients, in very short periods of time.

Even today, we owe our ability to hang a shingle outside our door and practice hypnotherapy, primarily because of the efforts of this performance arm of the hypnosis community. The reason I say this is because most people get their first exposure to hypnosis through comedy stage hypnosis shows, where they get to observe, and sometimes experience firsthand, the power of hypnosis and the subconscious mind. Armed with this new knowledge they may then seek out a local hypnotist to help them with their goals.

With this understanding of the value that street and stage hypnosis offers for raising public awareness of hypnosis, I believe it only proper to spend some time discussing this aspect of hypnosis in more detail. If you decide to do street or stage hypnosis, I know from firsthand experience that you will find it to be one of the most rewarding and fun experiences of your life and it will help to generate not only an increase in your revenue stream, but an increase in your client stream as well.

What's the difference?

What's the difference between street hypnosis and stage hypnosis? Well, truthfully, not a whole lot, but there are some distinctions worth discussing. Street hypnosis is typically performed in public areas, streets, subways, malls, parks, any place where people gather in large numbers. For example, where you might find street performers like musicians, mimes, etc. even though these arts are very different from hypnosis, it's still a "performance" scenario that we're talking about here.

Stage hypnosis is usually performed at some venue and is marketed and built up over time, where tickets are sold or there is a door charge that people pay. Common places for stage hypnosis are bars, restaurants, theaters, high school prom and grad parties, corporate functions, county fairs and such.

With street hypnosis, it takes a lot of confidence to walk out into an area where there are a lot of people and then encourage people to step forward and be hypnotized. If you're short on experience and or confidence, then street hypnosis is a great way to build up both, very quickly.

Getting Started with Street Hypnosis

Ok, so once you have decided to do some street hypnosis, it's fairly easy to get started. But, before you go out in public, you will want to check your local laws to see if there are any specific "street performer" permits you need to get in order to perform in public areas. Once you figure out if it's legal to do so, and you have obtained the appropriate permits, then make a self-standing sign that says "Fee Hypnosis Today Only" and set it up somewhere in the park or mall or anywhere there is a high level of foot traffic.

It might be easier for you to attract "volunteers" if you have a friend there filming you or if you go out with a group of other hypnotists and are all out there working together. Once you get one or two people there participating in demonstrations, you'll soon draw a crowd. It's always amazing to me, but it seems like the somnambulists are always the first ones to volunteer. They're attracted to hypnosis like moths to a flame, which is great because it makes your job that much easier.

Once you get a volunteer, start off easy, don't try to do instant inductions right away, unless you have a volunteer who has been hypnotized before, start off with a nice rapid induction, like the Dave Elman induction and do some simple convincers, like eye lock or hand clasp. These will be the easiest to start off with and make for an impressive demo.

Remember, the people watching most likely know nothing about hypnosis, so even the simplest phenomenon will be amazing to them. In fact, it seems like the biggest crowd pleaser is when you do fractionation, where you have the subject open their eyes, you say "Sleep!" and they drop back into a deeper state. This seems to always get a big rush out of the crowd.

Once you get going, it pretty much drives itself. Work with one volunteer, then move on to the next, then the next, and so on. Make sure you have plenty of business cards to hand out and most importantly...have fun!

Getting Started with Stage Hypnosis

A Stage Hypnosis show requires more planning and organization than a street hypnosis outing, but the returns are much greater. A properly marketed and executed Stage Hypnosis show can pull in anywhere from $1,000.00 to $5,000.00 or more for a 60 or 90 minute show...not too bad.

Much like street hypnosis, it doesn't take much experience or training to get started doing stage hypnosis. A couple of simple group inductions, some suggestibility tests and a few skits are all you need to put on a show.

The secrets to putting together a great show, that keeps audiences coming back again and again, are first and foremost to keep the participants safety as your top priority; Develop shows that are appropriate for all ages; Make the shows entertaining and fun; Don't do anything that your volunteers will be embarrassed to tell their friends about the next day.

When planning your show, you can find many different examples of skits to perform on the internet. Simply enter "Stage Hypnosis Skits" into your favorite search engine and pick out the ones that you enjoy the most. Another great resource is the "The New Encyclopedia of Stage Hypnotism" by Ormond McGill. This classic book on stage hypnosis is filled with priceless knowledge and technique, and, in my opinion, is a "must have" for anyone interested in stage hypnosis.

Structuring a Show

Whether you're performing street hypnosis or a stage show, the basic structure of a performance is the same:

1. The self-intro.
2. The intro to your show.
3. Calling up volunteers.
4. Suggestibility tests with the volunteers.
5. A little induction to have the whole ritual.
6. Run your scripts.
7. Bring everyone out and end the show.

Setting up the Stage

When setting up your stage area, you want to make it as safe as possible for your volunteers. You may not be able to take all of these precautions all the time, especially for impromptu shows, but you should try to do as many as possible whenever you can.

When you line up the chairs for your volunteers, place the chairs flush against each other to reduce the chance of "pinch" points between the chairs. If you can, tie the chairs together, this will keep the volunteers from moving the chairs around and will also protect against someone leaning back in their chair and falling over.

Make sure there is plenty of room in front of the chairs for your volunteers, if you plan to have them standing and acting out skits during the show. Make sure there is plenty of room behind the chairs so that you and/or your assistant (if you have one) can safely walk behind the chairs to work with the volunteers.

Check all of the pathways to and from the chairs to make sure that aisle ways are clear of any trip hazards. Tape down any cables that may be present for lighting or camera work. If you're using a microphone, use a wireless microphone if at all possible, again to reduce the risk of a trip hazard.

For female volunteers, keep a look out for short skirts and make sure that they are seated in a manner that their dignity is preserved. If a female volunteer is always self-conscious about their skirt riding up or "voyeurs" in the front row, they won't be fully concentrating on you, which will affect their ability to go into trance.

Make a point to have everyone spit out any gum they are chewing, provide them with a cup to dispose of the gum prior to starting your group induction. Don't let volunteers bring their drinks on to the stage. If they are wearing big hats that could interfere with other volunteers, ask them to remove the hat before starting the show.

If someone has been drinking too much, to the point that they are staggering drunk, then don't let them volunteer, they won't be good participants and they pose a risk to other participants. Don't let pregnant women or people with obvious injuries volunteer, because they may be at risk of injury on stage.

Most of these things are fairly common sense, and it's important to go over them so that you can create a safety "check list" for your show. Remember "Safety, safety, safety."

The Introduction

Whether you're performing street hypnosis or a stage show, the introduction of yourself and your show is very important. Always write your own introduction, especially if someone else is going to introduce you. Your introduction is where your credibility and authority is established for the context of the performance.

After being introduced to the audience, your "pre-talk" is the most important part of your show. This is where you will dispel myths and misconceptions about hypnosis. During your pre-talk, you will inform the audience that you will take care of them and that their safety and well-being are your top priority. Let them know that everything that happens on stage is completely natural, and that you won't have them do anything that they would be embarrassed to tell their friends about.

Calling for Volunteers

Let's face it; unlike singers, dancers or magicians, a hypnotist has no show without volunteers. If you don't get any volunteers, then your "show" becomes a "lecture", which is ok, but usually not what people want to see.

So, how do you get people to volunteer? As it turns out, it's really not that difficult. There is a natural curiosity when it comes to hypnosis, so many times you will get volunteers, simply by asking for them. Other times it will take only a little bit of coaxing.

When people are reluctant to volunteer, it's because they still have some fear or uncertainty, so if your pre-talk is done properly, then these concerns will have already been met. Plus, you have to contend with the issue that no one wants to be the "first" to volunteer, but once one person comes up, you will soon get others.

The rate at which people volunteer, and the number of volunteers, can vary drastically depending on the demographics of your audience. If you are performing for a high school or college age crowd, you will most likely get more volunteers than you can handle. This younger demographic is much more open to the prospect of a "reality altering" experience, and hypnosis is a safe and easy way to experience it.

If you are working with an older crowd, or a corporate crowd, then you will usually have to coax them a little more, mainly because of the fear of looking silly in front of their friends or co-workers. It may be helpful to get one person to "assist" you with demonstrating a group suggestibility test. Have that person stand on stage with you and demonstrate to the audience what to do as you talk them and the audience through the test. Once the test is completed, keep them on stage as your first volunteer, this will clear the way for others to volunteer, now that someone is already on stage.

If you always treat your volunteers with respect and dignity, then your reputation will grow in a positive way, and you will find that people are more eager to volunteer at your shows. Remember, no one wants to be made a fool.

A good way to prime the crowd for volunteers is to do a group suggestibility test, like the "magnetic fingers" followed by the "light and heavy hands". These group tests also allow you the opportunity to identify the potential somnambulists in the crowd. Get a few of those to volunteer and you're practically guaranteed to have a great show.

Kicking off the Show

Now that you have your stage full of volunteers, it's time to kick off the show. Thank the volunteers for coming up and get the rest of the audience to applaud and cheer them on as well. Continuously convey to the volunteers that they will be safe and that you will look after them. Frequently praise the volunteers as to how well they are doing. Everyone wants to feel they are doing a good job, and by frequently acknowledging this, you increase the volunteer's confidence and willingness to participate.

Begin your show with another group suggestibility test with the volunteers on stage. If you get a good response, you can easily convert this into a group induction. You'll want to check out who is being compliant and who is not. The best rule of thumb is to dismiss people early and often, and keep only the best subjects on stage. Remember, this is not therapy, this is entertainment, and you only want to keep the best of the best for your show.

The group induction of the volunteers is as much a part of the show as anything else, so make it a big deal, and entertaining. Inform the audience that you need their cooperation to be as quiet as possible during the induction so that you can prepare the volunteers for the show. Let them know that at the conclusion of the induction, the audience is free to make as much noise as they want.

Take your volunteers through the group induction and deepen them, give them your boilerplate suggestions about the noises around them helping them to go deeper, and that your voice will stay with them, and the safety of the chair, etc.

Progressing the Show

There's a natural progression to a show, and each suggestion builds on the one before it, creating depth and compliance. Start off with simple skits, with the participants' eyes closed, like suggesting hot and cold, or watching a sad or funny movie. These suggestions are the easiest phenomena to create, and help to guide the volunteers deeper into hypnosis. Remember to praise the participants often and encourage the audience to do the same.

While doing the group skits, start to identify the more "animated" members of your group of volunteers. These will be the stars of your show. After the simple group skits, start introducing the more entertaining individual skits, or group skits, made up of your "stars". You can suggest things like "name amnesia" or getting "stuck" to their chair, or every time you say a certain word or phrase they become excited or irritated.

The key, when progressing through the show, is that you never formally bring your participants out of hypnosis. You tell them to open their eyes and interact, and that when you snap your fingers, or say the word sleep, that their eyes close and they go back into trance again. They are never really out of trance until you do the formal wake up process at the end of the show. However, the audience doesn't know this, so every time you snap your fingers, and their eyes close, it creates a fascination for the audience.

You can suggest random skits, or you can create a progression of skits that tell a story, either way, your audience will be entertained.

Wrapping Things Up

When ending your show, always remember to remove all of the suggestions that you gave your participants during the show, and test to ensure that the suggestions have actually been removed. Then give them a "hypnotic gift" before finally awakening them. Give them suggestions of increased confidence and self-esteem, or give them the suggestion of a good night's sleep, really, any positive suggestions for well-being are a good post hypnotic suggestion to give participants as a "thank you" for volunteering. This is what I mean when I say "hypnotic gift".

At the end of your show, while the audience is still in awe over your performance, is a great time to pitch your products and services. Shows generate a lot of business for a hypnotist, so take full advantage of this marketing opportunity.

Protect Yourself and Your Participants

Even if you take all of the necessary precautions in your show, accidents can still happen, so it's important to have the proper professional liability insurance before you begin to perform public shows.

Most agencies will require a certification of completion of a stage safety course, and many of them offer access to such courses. Not only is it mandatory for most agencies, I highly recommend it to anyone planning to present public shows and demonstrations. Again, the safety of our participants is our TOP priority.

Getting the Gigs

So you want to perform, you know how to hypnotize individuals and groups, you've studied skits and techniques that you have found online or in books, or picked up at actual live shows of other hypnotists...how do you book a show, and where?

Well, this is where you have to break out of your comfort zone a bit and knock on some doors. You can find opportunities at clubs, restaurants, theaters, high schools and colleges, and corporations. How you get them is either by self-promoting or getting an agent to help you find work.

Parties and Gatherings

The easiest way to get started is by doing "impromptu" shows at parties and gatherings. At first you won't be getting paid for these, because they are spontaneous, unplanned shows. These are easy to do and are a lot of fun, not to mention a great way to build up experience, confidence and technique.

When you're at a party or gathering (unless it's a funeral or wake, then maybe not) and you are mingling with the crowd, casually mention that you are a hypnotist and ask if they would like to try something really cool. Some people will shy away, but many of them will be completely fascinated by the idea (remember, most people have little knowledge about hypnosis beyond TV and the movies). Show them some simple suggestibility tests to pique their interest.

When you begin working with one person, you will usually start to gather a small crowd and then, suddenly, you are no longer just another guest at the party, now you're "The Hypnotist". Begin doing suggestibility tests with other people, or a group of people. This can easily be escalated into a mini-show.

Parties and street hypnosis, at parks or night clubs, are a great way to get a lot of experience really quickly.

Conclusion

Well, I hope you enjoyed this book and were able to obtain the knowledge not only to increase your understanding of hypnosis, but to start you on your journey to really applying the techniques described herein.

Hypnosis is a powerful tool for good in this world, and we need more people to be aware of its power, and to begin applying it in every area of their lives, not only to improve their own lives, but to improve the quality of life for everyone around them as well.

As with all things, you get better with practice, so find a friend to share the journey with you, and get out there and practice the techniques covered in this book. Start off by doing simple inductions, with suggestions to instill confidence, and to build self-esteem. Before getting into more "heavy" issues, make sure you have enough experience to deal with any issues that may arise.

I have endeavored to make this book as thorough as possible, but the field of hypnosis is far too vast to put into a single book. There are many great teachers out there, and a lot of varying opinions, some of which will conflict with those expressed in this book, but that's ok. Find the teachings that fit with your beliefs, and which are adaptable to your own unique views and personality, and share what you learn with others.

I truly believe that the only true path to mastery is through teaching, so I encourage you to teach what you learn with others, and I thank you for helping me on my own personal journey toward increased mastery.

With that said, I am continuously learning and adjusting to what I learn, and I value all feedback, both praise and structured criticism. If you want to share your opinions of this book with me, then I would love to hear from you, just send your comments to:

info@HypnotistMichaelWhite.com.

I try to respond to all the email I get, and I get a lot, so please be patient with me if it takes a while to get back to you. Let me know how you are applying what you learned in this book. Also, if you run across any innovative uses of hypnosis, then please, by all means, share, I'm always open to learning new things.

Take care and enjoy.

Appendix A

Sample Intake Form

Client History

Session Date: _____

Name: _____ Address: _____ City: _____

State: _____ Zip: _____ Phone: _____ Cell: _____

Date of birth: _____ Age: _____ Sex: _____ Marital Status: _____

Employer: _____ Title: _____

How did you hear about us? Yellow Pages: _____ Newspaper: _____

Referral: _____ Name: _____ Doctor's Name: _____

Other:

_____

Medical History

Have you been under a doctor's care in the past year? Yes ____ No ____

If yes, please give reason: _____ Doctor's Name: _____

Are you pregnant? Yes ____ No ____

Have you ever been treated for an emotional problem? Yes __ No __

Have you been diagnosed with Asthma? Yes ____ No ____

Are you Diabetic? Yes ____ No ____

Are you currently receiving treatment or counseling? Yes ____ No ____

Do you have a heart condition? Yes ____ No ____

Have you been diagnosed with Epilepsy? Yes ____ No ____

If you answered yes to any of the above, please provide details: _____

Please list any medications you are currently taking: _____

Reasons for taking medication: _____

Reasons you are coming for hypnosis: _____

Any previous efforts to solve the problem? Yes ___ No ___ Results _____

Are you currently undergoing medical or psychological treatment for the above problem? Yes ___ No ___

Where? _____Doctor's Name: _____

_____   _____
Signature   Date

Appendix B

Boiler Plates

Boiler Plate 1 (BP1)
- Sounds around you
- My voice follows you
- Sanctuary (Feel the chair beneath you, you know you are safe)

Boiler Plate 2 (BP2)
- Ease of re-induction
- Self -Esteem
- Good Work

BP1 should be used right after putting someone into hypnosis

Sounds around you
"From time to time you may hear noises around you; these are just the normal noises of everyday life and will not disturb or bother you in any way. In fact, these noises will only help you to go even deeper, as you concentrate only on the sound of my voice, and my voice takes you deeper."

My voice follows you
"My voice will follow you on this journey of deep and profound hypnosis and the meaning of my words will stay with you at all times."

Sanctuary
"Notice the chair you're sitting on, feel it press up against you, notice how it supports you fully, and know that you are safe. And at any time you need to return to this place of safety, simply feel the chair beneath you and you will know you are safe."

BP2 should be used just before counting someone out of hypnosis

Ease of re-induction
"Now, each and every time you choose to go into hypnosis, you'll find that you go in quicker, easier and deeper each and every time. And anytime I suggest sleep to you, for the purpose of hypnosis, with your permission, you will enter hypnosis quickly and easily, to this depth or even deeper, each and every time."

Self Esteem
"You are a wonderful person, a person of worth, a good person, someone who cares for others and is cared for, an amazing person who is a joy to be around."

Post Hypnotic Praise

"You did an excellent job today. You demonstrated amazing intelligence and remarkable imagination, which means that you have made many wonderful improvements in your life."

Appendix C

Sample Progressive Relaxation Script

Sit back in your chair. Uncross your legs and arms, feet flat on the floor and arms resting comfortably on your legs or the arms of the chair. Now close your eyes. Now begin taking five deep breaths and with each breath you exhale, you will find yourself relaxing more and more. You may even begin to feel heaviness in your body, or a feeling of sinking, this is normal and will only help to relax you even more.

[After observing the client taking the fifth deep breath, begin the relaxation patter.] Concentrate on your feet; notice the heaviness of your shoes on your feet. You will begin to feel heavy, and this heaviness turns into relaxation in your toes and your feet. With each breath you exhale, notice how the relaxation moves from your toes and feet to your heels and the ankles on your feet. You are now feeling this heavy, calming relaxation move up from your feet into the calves of your legs...feeling the heaviness pushing your legs down, heavier and heavier...feeling your legs relaxing deeper and deeper relaxed.

And this relaxation moves upward into your knees, thighs and hamstrings, now, as you concentrate on the sound of my voice, and my voice guides you deeper and deeper into relaxation.

[This is a good place to inject some boilerplate patter. Boilerplates will be discussed in more detail later on. Here is the "sounds around you" boilerplate patter.] From time to time you may hear other noises around you. These are just the noises of everyday life and will not disturb or bother you in any way. In fact they will only tend to help you relax more deeply, as you concentrate only on the sound of my voice, and my voice, and the meaning of my words, follows you as you go deeper and deeper relaxed, now. *[The "sounds around you" patter is important, because if there should be some sudden noise, like a phone ringing or a noise from traffic outside or anything, it could startle the subject and cause them to lose concentration and perhaps bring them out of trance. In this way, we use these noises to our advantage, by having the client ignore them and allow them to relax them further.]*

Now feel the relaxation moving upward into your thighs and hips and into your lower abdomen and lower back...the relaxation continues to move upward to your mid-section, your stomach, back and chest, so that your entire body and torso become saturated with this heavy, deep, feeling of relaxation.

Your breathing becomes very deep, gentle and rhythmic, and a deep relaxing feeling, like daydreaming takes over...LETTING GO! Drifting down more deeply and deeply relaxed.

You may begin to feel a numb, pleasant, tingling feeling in your fingers and hands, as the relaxing feeling flows through your fingers and hands and into your forearms. The relaxation continues to move upward into your upper arms, biceps and shoulders, relaxing all of the tension in your shoulders and upper back.

The relaxation moves up from your shoulders into your neck, relaxing the neck muscles...completely relaxing...letting go. And that deep, heavy, relaxing feeling now, moves up the back of your neck to your scalp and the top of your head and down over your face, relaxing all the muscles in you scalp and face...completely relaxing now.

The relaxation moves down over your forehead and down over your eyelids. Your head begins to tilt downward toward your chest as your neck and shoulders release their tension and you relax more and more...completely relaxed...letting go.

And as I count from five down to zero, each count will represent deep relaxation, and you will feel your body relaxing more and more...deeper and deeper...and when I reach zero, you will go deeply asleep. Now, FIVE...letting go...FOUR...THREE...TWO...ONE...ZERO *[snap your fingers when you say "zero" and say]* DEEPLY ASLEEP!

[Now redirect the client's attention by saying] Now concentrate on my voice, and my voice will guide you more deeply asleep, with each and every gentle breath you exhale.

[Now you can do any change work the client requested, or in the case of practice, end with some "feel good" suggestions and emerge them. Here's a "sleep good" boilerplate patter I like to use, along with a "feel good" emerging patter] When you go to sleep tonight, at a time of your choosing, you'll find that you fall to sleep quickly, sleeping deeply and soundly, having the best sleep of your life, waking up, at the time you desire, feeling rested, refreshed and revitalized, ready to face the new day with excitement and vigor. And in your early morning dreams, you

will vent out any remaining issues that, in the past, may have caused you anxiety or concern...just letting go.

In a moment, I will count from zero up to five, and on the count of five, and not beforehand, you will awake, feeling fully alert and absolutely fantastic. Starting with zero [snap your fingers] we always go a little bit deeper, one, the blood beginning to flow more freely through your veins...two, becoming more aware of your surroundings, the chair your sitting on, the clothes against your skin...three a really powerful feeling of wellbeing beginning to build inside of you...four, that good feeling becoming stronger with each breath you inhale. So strong that you have a tendency to smile...and with the next number that urge to smile becomes irresistible and...FIVE, Eyes open, and wide awake, feeling absolutely fantastic.

Appendix D

Sample David Elman Induction

Start off by having the subject(s) sit in a safe and secure position. If I feel that the seating is not to my preference in this area (like folding chairs in a group session or workshop) I'll often make the waking, pre-hypnotic suggestion that "At all times you will remain safe and secure in your chair."

Let's begin with three deep breaths. Now, breathe in and hold it for a second, and as you exhale, begin to feel your body relax. Now take another deep breath and hold it a little longer...now exhale. Now, take one more really deep breath and this time, as you exhale, allow your eyes to close. That's right, you're doing great.

Now focus your attention on the small muscles around your eyes and your eyelids. Imagine that your eyelids are so relaxed that they will not open. Want it to happen; Let it happen; I can't do it for you, only you can make it happen. Relax those eyelids so completely that they will not open. And only when you are convinced that they will not open, I'll have you give them a little try and find that they remain closed tight. Now, give them a try and find them stuck tight...*[if they subjects eyes remain closed then you have the effect you're looking for and you can continue on. If they pop open, then you can tell them...]* you have proven that you can move tension back into your eyes and allow them to open, you control this, just as I said. Now let's see if you can relax them to the point where they remain closed. Let's try again...close your eyes... *[Now repeat the patter about relaxing the eyes and test again. At this point the subjects eyes will normally remain shut]*...That's great. Now stop trying and go deeper. *[When the subject's eyes remain closed, then you have achieved catalepsy of a small muscle group which is an indication of a light stage of hypnotic depth]*.

Continue to hold on to the relaxation around your eyes, and take a deep breath, and as you exhale, allow that relaxation to wash over your entire body, from the top of your head, down to the tips of your toes, relaxing every muscle and fiber in your body...completely letting go.

Now I'm going to lift your right hand by grabbing your thumb. Now I know you can lift your arm, but today let me do all of the lifting. Let your arm be loose and limp like a wet rag. *[Grab the subject's right thumb and lift the arm up. You're looking for any tension here. If tension exists, tell the client to give you all of the weight and to relax the arm...let you do all the lifting.].* When I drop your hand, when it touches your leg, send another wave of relaxation over your entire body, from the top of your head; to the tips of your toes *[now drop the subject's hand on to their thigh. It doesn't need to be far, just a few inches, but the act of dropping it will create a sinking feeling in the subject, creating a deepening affect].*

Now I'm going to lift your left arm in the same way and when I drop it on your thigh, send another wave of relaxation over your entire body, from the top of your head; to the tips of your toes. *[Repeat the arm drop with the left arm].*

Now, your body is relaxed and I'm going to show you how to relax your mind. In a moment I'm going to have you begin counting out loud backwards from 100 and after each number, you'll say the words "deeper relaxed". This is how you'll do it *[demonstrate for the subject what you want them to do]* "100...deeper relaxed...99...deeper relaxed" and so on. I want you to allow the numbers to fade from your mind, so that by the time you reach 95, or even sooner, they will be completely faded away.

Now begin (subject "100...deeper relaxed") you're doing great. (Subject "99...deeper relaxed") now begin to let the numbers fade (subject "98...deeper relaxed") make them a burden that you want to get rid of. Want it to happen, let it happen, feel it happen (subject "97...deeper relaxed") almost gone now (subject "96...deeper relaxed") and on the next number now, just push those numbers completely out of your mind ("95...deeper relaxed") *[often the subject won't make it this far in the numbers, usually around 97 the subject will find it difficult to find the numbers or to even speak. When the numbers fade, you have achieved a level of hypnotic amnesia, which is an indication of early stages of somnambulism].*

If there are any numbers left, don't worry, they will continue to fade as you breathe, and each gentle breath you exhale will double the relaxation you feel right now. *[Now continue on with your deepener].*

Appendix E

Questions about why you smoke

1. Do you smoke because of anger or boredom?
2. Is handling or watching the smoke part of the enjoyment?
3. Do you think smoking is pleasant and relaxing?
4. When you run out of cigarettes do you find it almost unbearable until you get some?
5. Do you smoke cigarettes automatically without even being aware of it?
6. Do you smoke to stimulate or perk yourself up?
7. Do you get a real gnawing hunger for a cigarette when you have not had one recently?
8. Do you often find a cigarette in your mouth and not remember putting it there?
9. Do you smoke at work as a means of getting away for a few moments?
10. Do you smoke at home as a means of getting away for a few moments?

Questions about motivation

1. Why do you want to stop smoking?
2. Do you really want to stop?
3. How many cigarettes do you smoke each day?
4. Do you smoke them all the way down?
5. What brand do you smoke?   (for nicotine level)
6. At what age did you start smoking?
7. Have you stopped and started again before?
8. How did you stop?
9. How easy or hard was it to stop then?
10. What made you start again?
11. When do you smoke?
12. What are the triggers?
13. What do you like and dislike about smoking?
14. Do you have any fears about stopping smoking?
15. Are there times you can go many hours without smoking and it does not bother you?

Made in the USA
Charleston, SC
30 June 2011